The 2020 Portland Riots

A Fight against Domestic Terrorism

An Officer's Memoir

Tommy Clark

The 2020 Portland Riots
Copyright © 2022 by Tommy Clark

The views and opinions expressed in this book are those of the
author and do not necessarily reflect the official policy or position
of McHenry Press.

Published by
McHenry Press
www.McHenryPress.com
"Let's bring your book to life!"

Library of Congress Control Number: 2022902371

Paperback ISBN: 978-1-955043-67-0

Typeset by Art Innovations (http://artinnovations.in/)
Cover design by Debbie Lewis

Printed in the United States of America

This book is dedicated to the brave men and women of law enforcement, the true guardians of peace. Thank you for your dedicated service to protect people from those who would exploit the weak and vulnerable. A profession that protects all, regardless of race, religion, or color. A profession ever vigilant that continues despite weekends, holidays, or adverse weather. For those who have made the ultimate sacrifice, you will never be forgotten. We will honor your memory through hard work and dedication, and we will continue to protect those who cannot protect themselves. To my brothers and sisters at the Portland Police Bureau, I am proud to serve with each and every one of you. May courage and integrity be the foundation of your personal and professional life.

CONTENTS

Introduction   1

Chapter 1: Coming Home   3

Chapter 2: George Floyd   15

Chapter 3: Officer Meets Linda Blair   24

Chapter 4: Little Man in the Park   30

Chapter 5: The Fence Line   39

Chapter 6: Operation Snatch and Grab   45

Chapter 7: Gun Violence Reduction Team (GVRT)   60

Chapter 8: The Siege of East Precinct   64

Chapter 9: Concrete Justice   80

Chapter 10: The Long Wait   94

Chapter 11: The Civil Lawsuit   105

Chapter 12: Criminal Investigation Analysis   113

Appendix: Memorandum from Deputy DA
          Nicole Hermann to DA Mike Schmidt
          Regarding PPB Office Thomas Clark   126

Notes   136

About the Author   139

CONTENTS

INTRODUCTION

The death of George Floyd on May 25, 2020, stimulated violent demonstrations in many cities in the United States and other parts of the world.

During the summer of 2020, I served as an officer on the front lines of nightly riots in Portland, Oregon. Eventually, a confrontation with a rioter and a viral YouTube video led to my temporary removal from the streets.

You may even have watched the video.

The 2020 Portland riots were among the worst riots ever experienced in our great nation, and they were by far Portland's longest-running protest.

For more than a hundred consecutive days, the nightly disappearance of the sun became a symbol of the violence and destruction that awaited the city as Antifa and Black Lives Matter (BLM) groups lay siege to the community through arson, vandalism, and looting.

Night after night, the brave men and women of the Portland Police Bureau and other agencies risked their lives to prevent the complete destruction of Portland at the hands of extremist groups.

What really happened on the streets of Portland during the riots of 2020?

What monumental failures of city leaders gave rise to unprecedented levels of violence that rocked Portland in 2020 and continue to ravage the city?

How do law-abiding citizens bring about the kinds of changes critical to the health and survival of our nation?

This my story . . .

CHAPTER 1

COMING HOME

March 1, 2020

I am finally leaving Fort Lewis, Washington, after spending twelve months in physical rehabilitation.

After loading my belongings into my truck, I look back at the barracks for a few seconds before speeding off toward the front gate. In two hours I will be home, and tonight I will sleep in my own bed. The thought gives me comfort for a moment. Then a bittersweet feeling of nostalgia overcomes me as I begin to look around the old barracks by the airfield.

At the stoplight, I could go straight and be outside the gate in three minutes or go left and the road will take me to the other side of the airfield. I decide to take a left and drive toward the old WWII barracks where I used to live as a young private in the army.

I get to the barracks, pull into the parking lot, and shut off my engine.

3

Sitting quietly in my car, I stare at the second-floor windows where my room used to be. Twenty-one years ago, I moved into these barracks with my two roommates. I was nineteen years old.

So much has happened in the last two decades.

I close my eyes.

* * *

After eight years of active duty mixed with activated Reserve time with CONUS and OCONUS assignments, I had transitioned to serve in the reserves as a "weekend warrior." The following year, in 2009, I'd been hired on at the Portland Police Bureau.

In 2017 the reserves unit I was in released me for a deployment to Saudi Arabia, and I served as the Director of Operations under the Ministry of Interior-Military Assistance Group (MOI-MAG). Our mission was funded by the country of Saudi Arabia through Foreign Military Sales (FMS) cases fulfilled by U.S. Army Security Assistance Command (USASAC). Our assignment: train and advise the Ministry of Interior's security forces on defending their critical infrastructure facilities and its people from terrorism.

Saudi Arabia has roughly thirty-four million people, and each year millions of Muslims travel from all parts of the world to take part in the Islamic religious holidays called Ramadan and Hajj. One of the world's largest movements of humans can be seen at the Grand Mosque in Mecca. The sheer number of pilgrims arriving simultaneously in Mecca is staggering, and the stress that it imposes on transportation and security is overwhelming. Security forces not only have to protect millions of people, but they are tasked to safeguard railways, airports, seaports, desalination plants, oil refineries, and pipelines. A daunting task if personnel are ill equipped or not properly trained.

Our team of less than one hundred instructors was displaced in three locations across Saudi Arabia. The command center was located at a small compound outside Riyadh, and the two training centers were located in Dammam and Jeddah. The nature of my work required me to devote 75 percent of my time and effort inside the operations cell or inside the diplomatic quarter in Riyadh. The other 25 percent took me to the training sights in Dammam and Jeddah.

I have driven in many places around the world, but nothing was more perilous than driving the chaotic freeways of Saudi Arabia. Every day that we exited the compound was a fight for survival against inexperienced and emotionally charged drivers. Driving in a convoy inside an armored vehicle provided some level of protection, but there was always a fear of colliding with vehicles traveling at a high rate of speed mixed with sudden stops and U-turns by drivers who missed their exits.

To break the busy operational tempo and to alleviate stress, I ran a jiujitsu program three nights a week inside a tent that reached 130 degrees Fahrenheit during the summer. Fortunately, I was able to acquire a few air-conditioning units to lower the temperature to a cool 100 degrees. Jiujitsu provided a good distraction from the highs and lows of deployments.

There were challenges, to be sure.

A few incidents sidelined me with multiple injuries—a separated shoulder, broken finger, injured right ankle—I spent twelve exhausting months in a place called the Warrior Transition Unit (WTU). Six months at Fort Bragg, North Carolina, and six months at Fort Lewis, Washington. My time at both locations was defined by physical therapy, group classes, and other activities provided by the program.

Each night as I lay in bed, I would think about my return to police work and the training I would have to take before going back on patrol.

* * *

I've been away before for military deployments, but this by far has been my longest absence from police work.

I'm glad to be going home.

A soldier walking by notices my vehicle and approaches on the passenger side. "Sir, can I help you?"

I look at his rank and name tag and say, "No, Private Smith, thanks for asking. I'm just a soldier stopping by to see where it all started for me almost twenty-one years ago. Have a good day, Private." I turn on my engine and drive away from the First Squadron Fourteenth Cavalry's parking lot. "Warhorse," part of the Third Stryker Brigade Combat Team, Second Infantry Division, is one of the best units I have ever been a part of.

Before long, I'm looking at Fort Lewis from my rearview mirror. Time to get home, soldier, you have been away for far too long.

I turn my radio to country music and point my truck south toward Vancouver, Washington, the last city in Washington State before crossing over into Portland, Oregon. The constant hum of the tires threatens to lull me to sleep, so I pull over to get Dutch Bros coffee midway into my drive. Maybe Susie is still working at my favorite stop, maybe not. I've been gone three years. Coffee girls normally last about a year at a coffee shop. My theory is that they get tired of the creepy customers who show up two to three times a day and don't even drink coffee. Now here's another dirty old man about to grab a cup of coffee.

No Susie.

Good. I don't need to come back later today and pretend I need coffee. I sip my coffee and listen to Luke Bryan sing about being drunk on a girl and high on summertime.

The drive takes me about two hours, and before I can finish singing "Tennessee Whiskey," I'm pulling into my long gravel driveway. With my windows rolled down I look around and see weeds and grass licking the lower branches of the trees scattered around the property. Overgrown weeds and Scotch broom are creeping toward my shed.

I slowly come to a complete stop in the middle of my driveway and exit my vehicle. I take steps toward a particular tree that was exactly my height when I left for my deployment. I stand next to the tree and notice that it is about two feet taller than I am now.

I take out my knife and cut the blackberry vines that have wrapped themselves around the base of the tree.

"I'll give you a better cleaning later, my friend," I promise the tree. "First I need to unpack and eat."

The results of three years of neglect will keep me busy for the next few months, maybe even a year. It's a small price to pay for having privacy and a place I can call my own.

I purchased the property in mid-2016 and constructed the house prior to my deployment to Saudi Arabia. Construction concluded two days before Christmas of 2016, and my mother and I moved in that same day. My father had died the previous year, and I didn't want my aging mother living alone. Before leaving for Saudi Arabia in June of 2017, I promised her that when I got home, I would build a home for her next to mine. Well, I am home now and it's time to follow through with that promise.

I drive into the garage, where my mother greets me with a hug and a few tears.

I take the next thirty minutes to unload my belongings into the house before throwing myself down on the leather couch. The smell of chicken adobo hits my nostrils, and my stomach immediately rumbles as my mouth begins to water.

"How does it feel to be back home, son?" My mother sits next to me on the couch. "You've been gone for a long time."

"Feels good to be home, Mom." I reach for her hand. "Yes, it has been a long time. I'll take about four weeks off before going back to work. There's a lot I need to do around the property."

The first purchase I make is a red riding mower from Home Depot. I'm so excited when I get it home that I mow for six hours straight. My property is starting to look like home again.

I spend the next four weeks visiting old friends, cutting down Scotch broom, weeds, and grass, and making preparations for the construction of my mother's new home.

Days turn to weeks, and before I know it, April 2, 2020, is right around the corner.

I take my last two days of freedom to work on my shooting skills with the steel targets I've set up at the back of the property.

Prior to deployment, I was averaging thirty minutes a day of steel target shooting before the start of each shift. I get a small amount of practice rounds from the Bureau, but most of my stockpile is from my own production center located in my garage. With my Dillon 550 progressive reloader, I can crank out a few hundred rounds in one hour. I practice dry firing and unholstering my pistol for the first ten minutes before loading my first eighteen rounds (one in the chamber and seventeen inside the magazine). It's slightly bigger than the Glock 19 I carried in Saudi Arabia, but the fundamentals of shooting remain the same.

I shoot the first eighteen rounds at a steady pace and watch the steel targets dance back and forth with each round.

My pistol locks to the rear, indicating I am out of ammunition, so I quickly drop the empty magazine and load a full magazine from my duty belt. I slap the bottom of the magazine to make sure it is seated properly and forcefully rack the pistol and chamber a single round inside the chamber. When done fluidly and correctly, this process can be executed in one second or less. I fire the second volley at a faster pace and transition to combat shooting. I engage multiple steel targets that are five feet apart while moving at an angle toward the targets. I shoot from kneeling positions and on my back to simulate situations I may find myself while on duty. I go through three hundred rounds of 9 mm ammunition before transitioning to my Colt AR-15 semiautomatic rifle.

During my fourth year on the street, I became a rifle operator; a couple of years later I became an instructor.

I cannot imagine patrolling East Portland without a rifle in my vehicle. The gangs that Jo Ann Hardesty, city council member, believes do not exist run rampant in the city of Portland. Most of them are armed and some with fully automatic weapons. Gangsters who self-identify as gangsters leave their mark all over the city, and yet Hardesty continues to preach that Portland does not have a gang problem. If Portland had to depend fully on her ability to problem solve and intellectually manage a city and its resources, it would not take long for criminals to take ownership of the city, and the entire police force would cease to exist, replaced by social workers. Luckily, the geographically elusive commonsense bug, although few and far in between, miraculously has made its way into city hall and temporarily halted some of the dangerous and selfish ideology that Hardesty has attempted to inject.

I go through similar drills with my AR and send about two hundred rounds downrange. The sun is high up in the sky, and I realize I am covered in sweat. I take the next thirty minutes to pick up my brass and put my steel targets back inside the shed. Sometime in the next couple of weeks, I will take the steel targets to a family's farm in Goldendale, Washington, and work on long-distance shooting with my .308. Distance shooting is not needed for a normal workday; however, it is a skill I want to maintain and improve.

April 2, 2020

I wake up and prepare my gear for my first day back at work. I load my truck and nervously drive to the East Precinct of the Portland Police Bureau. I was told the first couple of weeks would be utilized for administrative tasks and also for catching up on online training videos I have missed for three years, something I am not looking forward to doing.

I pull into the garage and park my truck at the upper level of the parking structure, near the entrance of the second floor. I walk straight to the locker room and drop my gear on the bench in front of my locker. I look at my vest that's hanging in front of my locker and see that it is covered with dust. The once black color of my vest is almost gray now.

With a sense of anticipation, I open my locker, and the first thing I notice is a sticker on the inside of the door: "Be polite, be professional, but have a plan to kill everybody you meet." It's a quote from James Norman Mattis, a retired U.S. Marine Corps four-star general nominated as secretary of defense by President Donald Trump. Nicknamed Chaos, he was a great leader who commanded respect, and respect he received.

I load my gear into my main locker and notice my backup pistol lying on the top shelf. She will definitely need a good cleaning and some lubrication before I take her out on her first night of patrol in the mean streets of Portland. Next to my pistol are stacks of notebooks I have collected over my last eleven years as a police officer. Neatly stacked in seven piles are the notes detailing almost every call to which I have been dispatched.

I pull the oldest of the notebooks from the bottom of the pile and start flipping through the pages. My very first call as a rookie was a bar fight in downtown Portland where six intoxicated males fought over a girl. Names, dates of birth, addresses, phone numbers, and details of many incidents are forever scrawled on the hundreds of pages of my pocket-size notebooks. I carefully slide the notebook under the first pile and begin to load my gear in a cubbyhole next to my locker.

I hear the door to the locker room swing open, and moments later I see a familiar face beaming with a smile. It's a fellow officer I've worked with for years.

"Tommy! What the hell, you're back, bro! Damn, man, you were gone for a minute."

"Yeah, brother, it's good to be back. It's been way too long. I'm looking forward to getting back on the streets and chasing bad guys."

The smile on his face fades as he shakes his head. "Man, it's not the same anymore, bro. We can't chase bad guys anymore. Can't even go after stolen cars. I know you love finding and chasing stolen cars, but we can't pursue anymore unless it's attached to a person-to-person crime. Stolen car by itself, you'll just have to wave and say good-bye. So now we have a lot of stolen cars in Portland driving around, and they know we can't pursue them."

I, too, shake my head in disbelief. Before I left for Saudi, we would be in pursuit of a stolen vehicle every night and sometimes two or three. Over the years, I developed a talent for finding stolen cars and being able to memorize multiple license plates of stolen cars. Every day I worked the streets,

I set a goal to recover a minimum of three stolen vehicles before the end of my shift. More often than not, I was able to achieve my goal. City and state politicians have found another way to discourage proactive policing, providing yet another avenue of escape for criminals.

Knowing the current trend in the country regarding policing, I suspect I'll be hearing about additional new restrictions.

I chat with the officer about new policies and the current climate of the Bureau. From what he tells me, I feel fortunate to have missed the reign of the former chief of police, Danielle Outlaw.

We end the conversation, and I walk to the sergeant's office to report for duty. The sergeant tells me I will be in front of a computer for the first week, reading and signing policies and directives that have been issued during my absence. I'll also be required to watch over fifty training videos followed by check on learning exams. The following week I'll report to the training division where I will conduct firearms training and review qualifications and patrol tactics.

"I know you're itching to get back on patrol." The sergeant gives me a reassuring smile. "Get through the videos—there are a lot of them—and complete your in-service training. Then pick a person you want to ride with on your first week of patrol, and we will make it happen."

I inform the sergeant that I want to stay on the afternoon shift (1600–0200) with Fridays through Sundays off.

"Yep, I am tracking." He nods. "You definitely have enough juice to have weekends off. You won't recognize eighty percent of the afternoon crew. A lot of them are just out of probation and wet behind the ears. They are all hardworking, though, and hungry, your kind of crew."

After shaking hands, I walk to my cubicle and park myself in front of the computer.

"Videos, directives, and exams," I say to myself as I take a deep breath and loudly exhale. Not quite the glorious first week of work I had envisioned, but when it comes to boredom I have been in more dire situations.

In 2007 I sat in a small airfield in Baghdad for seventy-two hours waiting for a flight that would eventually take me to Qatar. I spent most of my time throwing small gravel rocks against the T-Walls—twelve-foot portable steel-reinforced concrete blast walls—surrounding the waiting area of the airfield.

Videos and directives, bring it on. Instead of gravel rocks, I'll get some popcorn and turn this week into a video marathon.

CHAPTER 2

GEORGE FLOYD

May 26, 2020

I wake up to news anchors chatting about police officers from Minneapolis, Minnesota, who took a black man into custody, and during the arrest, the suspect passed away. The video shows a handcuffed man—later identified as forty-six-year-old George Floyd—lying facedown on the ground with an officer kneeling on what appears to be Floyd's neck.

My mother saw the news hours before I did.

"Son," she tells me, "this does not look good. You know people in Portland will riot over this."

"Yeah, the video definitely does not look good, but I have a feeling there's more to the video than what we are seeing. Let's wait for the facts to come out before we make any assumptions."

I have worked in law enforcement long enough to know that the media will deceptively edit videos to show only what

15

they want the public to see. This is normally done to capture the support and emotions of those who are weak-minded and easily influenced. From 2014 through 2015, the liberal media, Lebron James, and other groups propagated one of the biggest lies in the history of police shootings. It was a lie that ignited hatred and blatant attacks on police officers across the United States. It wasn't until March 2015 that a major liberal media outlet acknowledged that the "Hands up, don't shoot" movement was built on a lie. Based on forensic evidence and exhaustive interviews, it was proven that Michael Brown never surrendered with his hands up when he was shot by Darren Wilson.[1]

As I watch the video of George Floyd being played over and over, I quickly notice that events prior to or during the arrest of George Floyd are not being shown. Why is this person on the ground handcuffed? Was he resisting the officers during arrest? Were officers unable to get him into the vehicle? Was he intoxicated or high on drugs?

Questions continue to cultivate inside my head as I recall many instances where I've had to deal with someone who was either high on drugs or going through excited delirium. People who have never experienced any physical conflict (other than maybe fighting with an unresponsive remote control) fail to understand that even a handcuffed individual can pose significant threats to arresting officers by kicking, head butting, and biting. A person who is high on drugs or going through methamphetamine psychosis or excited delirium has phenomenal strength and low tolerance to pain. I have personally responded to multiple calls where we had to hold a person down with force in order to prevent self-inflicted injuries or injuries to others. Sometimes it would require four to five officers to hold down a drug-induced person until the sedative administered by medical personnel took effect.

Taking all of this into consideration as I watch the video of George Floyd, I can confidently bet that he was high on drugs and resisted arrest. Police officers do not usually force people on the ground unless they are resisting arrest or the subject must be positioned on the ground for officer safety and to avoid further escalation of force.

I head into work. There, I continue to hear chatter about the video of George Floyd.

An officer from the Riot Response Team (RRT) says, "Looks like we are activated for a possible protest on Friday. I'm pretty sure they are going to cancel days off for everyone the entire weekend."

In the past, Portland has been a main hub for demonstrations for all things unrelated to Portland. The liberal city's extreme tolerance for rioting and destruction has made it a haven for criminals and rioters. Occupy Portland in 2011 turned the city into a cesspool of drug activity and sexual deviance inside the camps. It also—and literally—turned the city into a sewer of feces, urine, and other bodily fluids. Demonstrators left behind tents, wooden structures, used needles, and more garbage than CNN or MSNBC and the like could ever spew in one day.

Many riots have followed Occupy Portland, and law enforcement days off are often canceled to combat the violence that accompanies most demonstrations in Portland.

Yet every election year the citizens of Portland vote the same incompetent and morally corrupt people into office.

The day goes on at work, and news of George Floyd continues to dominate social media and all the news outlets. I can already sense the hostility of some of the people on the streets as we drive by to patrol high-crime areas in East Portland.

The typical "Fuck you!"s and "Pigs!" have turned into silent stares and a finger gun to the head.

"This is not looking good," I tell my partner. "I think we need to prepare for a long weekend and possibly another Occupy Portland."

I finish the end of my shift with a feeling of uneasiness and fear of the days to come. A storm is brewing at a distance, but the coldness and devastation that it's going to bring can already be felt inside the locker room.

Videos like the one we've been watching all day will only incite violence toward law enforcement personnel. Many officers will lose their lives as they have in the past due to ignorance and hate-filled messaging by the liberal media and politicians. In 2019 the FBI revealed that eighty-nine police officers were killed in the line of duty that year. Forty-four of those officers were killed by way of firearms, and some of their murders were captured on video.[2]

These killings came as liberal media portrayed police officers as public enemy number one and propagated a narrative that white officers were systematically targeting black people across the United States. Their narrative completely ignored statistics, which showed that significantly more white people were shot by police than black people. Sadly, the truth is immaterial to the media when it challenges the narrative they want to disperse like a plague.

I leave the precinct and cautiously exit our parking structure. Sometimes people stand by the garage doors and film officers as they exit, capturing the license plates of the vehicles leaving the garage. Those pictures are to be posted all over social media.

I quickly get on the freeway and think about how much policing has changed just in the three years I've been away. City and state politicians have definitely restrained proactive policing by the policies and laws they have implemented. Criminals are emboldened and crime continues to rise at a level that will eventually be uncontrollable. As shootings continue to plague the city, Commissioner Jo Ann Hardesty is spearheading the effort to disband the Gun Violence Reduction Team (GVRT). Hardesty alleges that members of the GVRT disproportionately dedicate their efforts to stopping young black men of Portland. In other words, a civilian who knows nothing about police tactics and the importance of proactive policing is accusing a very professional group of officers of racial profiling. I fear that someday she will get what she wants and the people of Portland will suffer the consequences of her reckless and politically driven agenda.

I get home around 3:30 a.m. and find my mother sitting on the couch watching television. I can see the sadness and worry in her face as she watches the images on the screen.

More George Floyd.

I grab the remote and turn off the TV.

"Mom, it's late, you need to get some rest. Stop watching this stuff, it will only make you worry."

My mother sinks lower into the couch and says, "You need to be careful at work, son. It's going to get really bad for all officers in the country. I've been sitting here praying for you guys."

I thank my mom for her prayers and urge her to go to bed. I add, "I would love to talk to you about this, but it's very late. We can discuss more of this before I go to work tomorrow. But for now, please go to bed."

Oh, how the tables have turned! Years ago, she would tell me to go to bed because it was past my bedtime, and I had school in the morning. Now I'm telling my mother to get some sleep and to stop watching TV late at night.

Surprisingly, my mother walks to her room without any objection and closes the door. Two seconds later the door opens, and she says, "Oh, don't forget, I need a big closet for my house. I need space for my shoes, purses, and clothes."

Before I can answer her, the door closes again. I think to myself, *Well, Dad did the hard work of buying the shoes, purses, and clothes. I have the easy and less expensive part. I just gotta make sure her closet in the guest house is big enough to fit it all.*

I laugh quietly as I make my way into bed.

Before closing my eyes, I think of the George Floyd video and the coming storm. I hope I have the strength to endure the onslaught of evil in the form of disinformation and chaos that is to come. I say a prayer for all law enforcement personnel in the United States before falling into what I hope is a deep sleep.

The sound of the doorbell jolts me awake, and for a moment I don't know where I am. As I regain my bearings, I look at the clock.

Ten thirty a.m.

I'm not supposed to get up for three more hours. Based on the shift I work, this is the middle of the night for me.

What the heck! This better be good.

I throw on some clothes and walk to the front door with my eyes barely open. I open the door and see my friend John, a police officer from another department.

"Damn, dude," he says. "You look like shit, and you don't even drink at night . . . or day."

"I don't know what's brighter, the sun or you. Come inside before you get skin cancer."

John has always been pale and burns easily under the sun. His wife is always chasing him around with sunscreen and a honey-do list. Poor soul, no wonder he's at my house.

He sits on one of the bar stools.

"I'm guessin' you've seen the news about that black guy who died in Minneapolis. Is your department getting ready for a riot? I think there's going to be riots all over the country like the Rodney King riots in LA."

I tell John that our riot team is on standby and that our days off have been cancelled by the chief.

"Shit, man." He shakes his head. "If there's going to be a riot, it will definitely be in Portland. Criminals know they are protected in this city."

It's a bold statement but one I can't argue with.

We sit and talk for about an hour about what happened in Minneapolis, coming to the conclusion that the liberal media and politicians will turn this unfortunate incident into a race issue. There are people in this country who despise America and its core values so much that they want to make everyone believe America is a racist country. Yes, racism does exist in small pockets of the United States, but it is not rampant like the way corrupt media and politicians would make you believe.

I am a person of color who immigrated to the United States at the age of eleven, and I have never experienced racism. I have lived in many places in the United States, and I have yet to see an example of "systemic racism," a phrase commonly used by Democrats as a talking point during elections and disseminated by liberal news outlets. After all, the news never reports that "a man was shot by a policer officer." Instead, the story is always that "a white officer shot a black man." The media coverage in regard to officer-involved shootings of white people is significantly disproportionate to the coverage of black men being shot. The media is only interested in what will incite the public or what they can use as a catalyst to drive a political agenda.

And this sad reality has victimized law enforcement personnel in the United States and fueled the murder of many officers who wanted nothing more than to serve and protect those who cannot protect themselves.

As our conversation draws to a close, I have downed three cups of coffee and have abandoned any hope of going back to sleep.

"Tommy, you sure you can still do this riot stuff?" John asks as I walk him to the front door. "You just did a year of rehab. Plus you're an old man now." He grins.

"I'm only getting stronger and faster with age, brother. Now get out so I can hit the gym before work. Want to borrow an umbrella so you don't get burned by the sun on your way out the door?"

After John leaves, my thoughts return to George Floyd and the pending turmoil that is to come.

The media is hungry, and they have stumbled upon a feast that will keep them feeding for days to come.

CHAPTER 3

OFFICER MEETS LINDA BLAIR

Portland Riots, Day 15

On day 15 of the riots in downtown Portland, an eight-foot-tall chain-link fence line stretches one hundred feet or so around the Justice Center. It was erected after the attack on May 29, 2020, the first day of the riots, when thousands of people converged on the Justice Center condemning the death of George Floyd. The crowds set fires inside the ground level of the building. Many businesses were looted and vandalized. It was a night of mayhem that signaled the beginning of many more to come.

Every night since then, rioters have been gathering by the thousands in Chapman Park just west of the fence. Every night, attempts are made to scale or push the fence over. One person attempted to cut the fence with a wire cutter and was quickly introduced to a 40-millimeter rubber bullet. With a loud yelp he dropped the wire cutter and disappeared into the crowd.

For the last fourteen days we have stood side by side for hours inside the fence line, forming a human wall serving as the last line of defense for the Justice Center. Central Precinct of the Portland Police Bureau and the county jail both reside inside the Justice Center.

Tonight, Incident Command wants to try a different approach with the consistently violent crowd.

"The fence seems to be the center of their attention and the cause of their anger," a supervisor from Incident Command announces. "Let's try talking with them outside the fence. They see the fence as a sign of division so let's remove this factor and see what happens."

Outside the fence line?

I scan the park and tell my colleagues, "Tactically this is not a good idea. We absolutely have no protection if the crowd turns violent."

Following orders, we cautiously begin to walk the park outside the fence. The sun will be setting soon, and we search for bottles and rocks staged under shrubs or inside garbage cans to be used later as projectiles. With a fistful of rocks and bottles I walk over to the fence and hand the projectiles to an officer standing on the inside. We continue this process for about an hour.

As the sun begins to disappear over the horizon, the creatures of the night appear from the shadows. Dressed in black and looking like downhill mountain bikers, they begin to materialize out of the shadows.

Without warning we find ourselves face-to-face with a crowd of about three hundred people and growing.

I look around. I see signs saying, "Fuck the Police," "Quit Your Job," "I Can't Breathe," and so on. The crowd begins to form a half circle around my squad, and I instruct my squad to keep their backs toward the fence. Looking around the crowd, I feel the hatred and anger enveloping me like a blanket of fire.

I notice a man standing behind the crowd. He seems calm. Too calm. I can't see his hands. His hands are under his armpits and under his black leather jacket. Trying to ignore the verbal abuse coming from multiple directions, I try not to lose track of the calm stranger.

Now he is looking directly at me with piercing eyes full of hate and contempt.

I feel relief when my radio crackles with the familiar voice of one of the county deputies. "We got you guys. We are watching from the second floor."

County deputies armed with 40-millimeter, less lethal shotguns are perched on the second and third floor of the Justice Center, serving as an overwatch.

A white female who spent the last ten minutes screaming about police brutality takes a step forward and points her finger toward my chest.

I take a step back and tell her to wipe the foam from the corners of her mouth. Having a constructive dialogue with this person is not in my future, so I stand in silence.

She attacks with a barrage of racist insults and exposes me to words I know I will have to look up later in Urban Dictionary. With tears in her eyes, she describes the shame and suffering she has endured due to the systematic killings of black people by the hands of barbaric white police officers across the United States.

I take a step back and wait in silence as she continues screaming at me. I tell myself that this too shall pass. Eventually she will run out of things to say.

Abruptly, reality slaps me across the face. She's not running out of words or hate. How can someone talk so much, make absolutely no sense, and show no signs of fatigue?

It begins to feel as though the oxygen around me is being sucked out of the air. I take another step back with hopes of escaping the gravitational pull of the black hole that is threatening to swallow me.

"Lady," I say quietly with all the patience—and remaining oxygen—I can muster. "You have a lot of hatred in your heart. I will be praying for you."

Wrinkles suddenly appear on her forehead, around her eyes, and instantly I can feel the presence of evil. She looks right through me with dark, piercing eyes and says, "Fuck your Christianity, fuck your God, and fuck you."

I think of Linda Blair in the movie *The Exorcist* and for a brief moment expect to see this woman's head spin completely around before she covers me in vomit.

With a heavy heart I take a deep breath and slowly back away. I can't save this woman from the ignorance and stupidity that is ravaging and crippling this country. COVID-19, you've met your match.

The crowd continues to grow. Others are attempting to incite the crowd. I tell members of my squad that we need to peel back and retreat inside the fence before our avenue of escape is completely cut off.

I was wrong about this being a bad idea. It's a terrible idea.

As we retreat slowly back toward the entry point of the fence, the crowd follows. Inspired by the sight of retreating officers, they continue to push forward, chanting, "ACAB. All cops are bastards!" A few of us face the crowd as the rest of the squad walks through the small entrance of the fence. The last officer going through the fence pulls the back of my vest, and I walk slowly backward, still facing the hostile crowd.

The gate slams shut, and the crowd erupts into a celebratory yelling and clapping. Within seconds, bottles and rocks are flying through the air, almost hitting a fellow officer on the helmet.

A green laser beam hits my eyes, and I quickly close them and turn my head to the side.

I reopen my eyes, and the green laser is now harassing another officer to my right. Scanning the crowd, I spot the coward with the green laser. I give his description on the radio and spotlight him with my Polarion flashlight. He quickly ducks behind a tree and disappears into the crowd.

I direct my attention to the people standing closest to the fence, and I see the woman who told me to fuck my Christianity staring at me, her middle finger pointing straight up in the air. I stare back and expect more insults—but she is silent and unmoving like a statue.

I scan the middle of the crowd for weapons and projectiles. A young white female approaches the fence with her sign and presses it on the fence for us to see. The sign says, "Over fifty percent of police officers beat their wives."

A male officer to my right laughs and says to the young woman, "Obviously you don't know my wife very well. I'm the one who gets beaten if I step out of line."

She ignores his comment, looks at me, and says, "What say you, officer, do you beat your wife?"

"Not lately," I say with a straight face. "We've been too busy stopping people from burning down the city."

I sense that someone is staring at me. I can actually feel hate emitting from that person.

I look to my left and see "Linda Blair" still frozen in the same position, staring at me with her middle finger in the air. Then she lowers her finger, walks directly in front of me, and grabs the fence with both hands. I begin to seriously wonder if the woman is possessed.

"Pray for me?" she screams. "Fuck you! Pray for your fucking self, you fucking pig!"

She turns toward the crowd and disappears somewhere in the middle of the park.

The officer with the "abusive" wife turns to me and says, "Damn, Tommy, you must have really pissed her off. What the hell did you say to her?"

"I just told her I would pray for her."

"What? Are you serious?" He scratches his beard and says, "I wish someone would pray for me."

I punch him on the shoulder and say, "I'll pray that your wife stops beating you up."

CHAPTER 4

LITTLE MAN IN THE PARK

Portland Riots, Day 17

Chapman Park—a place protesters call "The Battlefield"—is where thousands of people have been gathering to express their opposition against what they believe to be police brutality and racism.

It's soiled not only with the blood and sweat of battle-hardened warriors but also with the saliva and stench of unemployed, ignorant millennials screaming, "Fuck the Police."

It's a place taken over by a generation out of touch with reality and blinded by insatiable rage and hate.

I scan the empty park with tired eyes. My helmet is heavy and it's narrowing my vision. I have not been able to apply gel to my hair in seventeen days, which is a tragedy unto itself.

It is five o'clock p.m., and the Battlefield remains empty of the degenerates who are probably still asleep in the basements of their parents' homes or on their phones finding ways to exploit the government's welfare system.

Today we find ourselves again combing the park in search of bottles, rocks, and any items that can be used as projectiles. Supply vehicles were seen earlier in the day dropping items in the park. One vehicle even dropped off a cooking grill and lawn chairs. I guess people get hungry after a night of rioting and looting. I've had everything thrown at me since the start of the riots—except a fat, juicy ribeye steak.

Something tells me to look inside the grill. Walking over, I pull up the grill cover and find five sixty-four-ounce bottles of charcoal lighter fluid.

"Pretty clever, but I'm not buying it," I say out loud.

I lower the lid to the grill and begin pulling the grill toward the precinct. I'm guessing disposing of these accelerants now will save at least a few businesses in Portland from being burned to the ground. I secure the grill behind the fence line, then slowly walk back toward the park.

People are filming and live streaming our every move. Someone is saying, "As you can see, the pigs are back at the park. Everyone start coming to the park."

I continue scanning the park for signs of blunt objects that I can carry back to the other side of the fence. The words *ALABAMA Crab Dangle*, scrawled in orange spray paint along the foundation of a downtown building, catch my eye. I feel sure this must be a country dance of some sort, but Google will educate me later.

With my helmet secure in hand, I close my eyes for a moment and try to imagine the beauty of the park before it was littered with garbage and disfigured with obscene graffiti.

Suddenly this rare moment of peace and serenity is shattered by the all-too-familiar war cry, "Fuck the police!"

Opening my eyes, I quickly secure my battle-scarred helmet and grab my baton with a speed only Bruce Lee can understand and appreciate. I scan the Battlefield expecting to see a group of angry protesters with their homemade shields and signs coming my way.

Nothing but emptiness.

Where did that voice come from?

I turn around and before me is a short, angry black man with a voice that matches his stature. Armed with his cell phone pointing toward me, he angrily squeaks, "Fuck you, pigs. I'm live streaming this shit. Hey everyone, come to the park and fuck with these pigs!"

"You need to move along," I tell him.

After exhausting all the words in his vocabulary, he crosses the street on his skateboard and continues to spew insults while live streaming. With a high-pitched voice he yells, "Fuck you, pigs. Nobody looks up to you, not even kids."

He continues to circle the Battlefield on his skateboard, chanting, "I hope you all fucking die, you fucking pigs."

Eventually, with his attention consumed by angry rhetoric and his live streaming, he loses his balance, hitting the ground and rolling a few times before stopping next to a flower bed. His skateboard rolls down the street.

At that moment, my sergeant walks over to the fallen man, leans over, and in a genuinely compassionate voice says, "Are you okay, little buddy?"

I bite my tongue to keep from laughing.

The man hops back on his feet and runs away with his skateboard under his arm. He stops just outside the park, raises his middle finger above his head, and yells, "You just wait for tonight! We are bringing everyone to the park!"

Another officer walks toward me and says, "You know he used to be a janitor inside the Justice Center? He was caught taking pictures inside the precinct and was warned about it, but he was caught again, so they got rid of him."

"Well, I'm glad he got fired. God only knows what he was doing with those pictures. I know Antifa and BLM are constantly walking around our precincts taking pictures from different angles."

Now the little man is walking up and down the middle of the street, yelling and grabbing his crotch. With his marbles in one hand, he displays the middle finger of the other and continues to dance in the middle of the street.

I figure if I arrest him now, I won't have to worry about him later.

As I take a step forward, I feel a strong grip on my shoulder pulling me back.

"Let him be, Tommy," the other officer tells me. "If we arrest him now, he'll just be out in two hours or less doing the same thing. The way he's dancing in the middle of the street, AMR may get to him before we do." AMR stands for American Medical Response—in other words, an ambulance.

33

He's right. Night after night we make arrests and many of the people we arrest are back on the street well before our shift is done.

I continue to stare at the jumping man as he taunts me with his Michael Jackson impression. I fight the urge to take him into custody before he gets hit by an unsuspecting driver who may not see him twerking in the middle of the street.

Instead, I take a deep breath. "You're right, we have bigger issues to deal with."

We walk slowly back toward the middle of the park.

"That's right, you little bitches," the man screams. "I'll be all up in your girlfriends tonight while you're at work."

I ignore the little man's immature taunting and give him a wave goodbye.

As I approach the chain-link fence that has kept these delinquents from burning down the Justice Center, I try to imagine what BLM and Antifa see as they gather in mass numbers armed with shields, blunt objects, and projectiles.

The fence has already withstood numerous assaults by angry mobs of BLM and Antifa. Rioters have tried to push down and dismantle the fence with heavy-duty wire cutters or handheld saws. A few brave souls have attempted to scale the fence before being pepper sprayed. Their hopes, along with their bodies, came crashing down like my grades in college after meeting the Johanson twins from Sweden.

The fence is strong, but it will not withstand thousands of angry people if they all push at once. I slowly walk alongside the fence checking the connection links and the wires. I

34

get to the other end of the fence and find myself face-to-face with a group of teenagers holding a BLM flag.

One approaches with his camera and says, "You all can't hide behind that fence forever, officers. We will eventually have that building and we will have your jobs."

I take a step closer toward the teenager in front of me and say, "Why don't you all be a productive member of this community and find a job. If you want our jobs, then go get educated and apply. Now, just like you guys, we have some planning to do for this evening."

I walk away from the group as they chant loudly, "Fuck the police!"

I rejoin the rest of my team in the middle of the park and continue to scan the area for possible threats. Across the street, the small angry man continues to taunt the rest of my team. Abandoning his Michael Jackson impression, he transitions to what I call the "new guy in prison" impression and pulls his pants down toward his ankles with his ass pointed toward all the officers in the park. After a few seconds of shaking his bare ass, he pulls up his pants and yells, "I hope you all die, you fucking pigs." He follows his grotesque act by thrusting both middle fingers up in the air and looks back to the crowd behind him for support and accreditation of his grand finale act.

The crowd erupts with laughter and yells, "All cops are bastards, all cops are bastards." This only emboldens the angry man, and he runs back and forth in front of the crowd with his balled fist up in the air.

I turn to my team and say, "All right, I've seen enough of the sideshow. Let's get ready for the evening. I'm sure we will run into him later. I hope we do."

We retreat back to our vehicles parked in front of the police precinct and prepare for the chaos that is looming. I strap a large can of pepper spray on my left leg and a gas mask on the other. We take the next thirty minutes to regroup, utilize the bathroom, and eat an early snack.

Just as I'm getting comfortable on the front passenger seat, the sergeant tells us to load up and prepare to stage outside the fence a few blocks away. With twelve officers in three vehicles we quickly leave the safety of the fenced compound and drive away from the Justice Center. I look out the window and see a few thousand people gathered just west of the fence line, completely saturating every square inch of the park.

We are now a Mobile Field Force (MFF), free to roam and to intercede where we are needed. We drive around the crowd, and I see people coming from all directions dressed in black and covered with knee and elbow pads. This is definitely not a sign of a peaceful protest, as our city leaders want us to believe.

Just then, the radio breaks silence and a sergeant informs everyone that officers inside the fence are taking multiple projectiles from the angry crowd.

A few seconds later a loud explosion sends a shock wave that triggers other explosions throughout the city.

The sergeant of the team inside the fence breaks another radio silence and screams, "We are taking mortars and other improvised explosive devices."

Incident Command tells the sound truck to declare an unlawful assembly and to give order of dispersal. A command that always seems to come a lot later than it should. Incident Command should immediately declare unlawful assembly the moment a projectile is thrown at police officers. Letting the crowd throw multiple projectiles at police officers for twenty to thirty minutes before taking action is completely irresponsible and shows the inability of Incident Command to take initiative.

A riot is finally declared, and the Riot Response Team springs into action and moves in from the south.

We exit our vehicles and move in from the east with other Mobile Field Forces to push the crowd west, away from the Justice Center. Somewhere in between the explosions, screaming, and vehicles honking, I hear a familiar voice. It's coming from somewhere behind all the smoke caused by burning dumpsters and CS gas released by the Riot Response Team.

"Put me down, you fucking pigs! Put me down."

The smoke momentarily clears, and I see two of the tallest officers of the Riot Response Team carrying the angry little man from the park by the armpits. I run to the officers and assist them in handcuffing the man. He continues to resist and throw insults at me and other officers, even claiming he was only being arrested because he was black.

I lower myself to look the race baiter in the eyes and say, "No, you're getting arrested because you committed a crime. Being black or brown is not a crime; otherwise, I'd be in handcuffs too. So stop perpetuating lies and start taking responsibility for your actions."

To my surprise he makes no effort to counter my remark and lowers his head toward the ground. For a brief moment the light emitting from the street lamp exposes the tears beading in the man's eyes, which I am sure he is trying hard to keep from escalating to a full-blown man cry.

I lay my hand on the man's shoulder. "Make better decisions, my friend, and I hope I don't see you again tonight."

I walk back to my team and continue to assist in pushing the violent crowd away from the park. With the help of State Patrol and a few other agencies, we clear the park in less than thirty minutes. The crowd is scattered, and small groups begin to vandalize and loot businesses in the downtown area. We spend the next four hours combating looters and fielding intermittent attacks directed toward the Justice Center.

The night ends with multiple arrests; however, though prosecution by District Attorney Mike Schmidt is unlikely.

Regardless of the DA's reluctance to hold criminals accountable, we will continue to defend businesses, critical infrastructures, and the citizens of Portland.

CHAPTER 5

THE FENCE LINE

Portland Riots, Day 20

The battle continues with no end in sight. Thousands of angry protesters gather daily with hopes of conquering the formidable fence. Behind the fence lies the all-imposing Justice Center, Central Precinct to the Portland Police Bureau, and a hotel for the many delinquents of Multnomah County.

Many of the protesters are platinum members of the Multnomah County Detention Center (MCDC). A group of professional rioters and criminals who have embedded themselves among peaceful protesters to conceal their nefarious motives. The fence line, as well as a few hundred brave men and women of law enforcement from multiple agencies, has kept these savages from defiling the Justice Center, a feat they were able to accomplish on day one of the riots.

It is almost midnight. The witching hour.

I stand with my back toward the Justice Center watching a group of approximately five thousand angry protesters with signs raised high. Spray-painted slogans include BLM, George Floyd, Fuck the Police, Defund the Police, and I Can't Breathe.

One message in particular catches my eye: "If you were the officer that pepper sprayed me last night, your mom is a ho."

I run my fingers over a half-empty can of pepper spray at my hip. Could the sign holder be the guy I pepper sprayed last night? It doesn't surprise me that he's already out of jail. How rude of me to offer this thirsty man only half a can. Maybe he will give me another opportunity later this evening to quench his thirst. As for my mother, she is a good, honest woman.

Unfortunately, officers are not the only ones armed with pepper spray. Many of the rioters are equipped with bear spray. I walked into a mist of it the other evening, and it ruined the rest of my night. I like spicy, but that was way too spicy.

A gentle breeze slowly passes through the night bringing a fleeting moment of relief from the humid air and heat trapped beneath my body armor and battle helmet. I look to my left and right and see men and women of the Portland Police Bureau ready to defend the Justice Center at all costs. I hear someone from the back yell, "Hold the line. If they break through the fence, this is where we make our stand, from that tree . . ."

The rest of the prebattle speech is muffled by the roar of the horde and their homemade shields pounding against the fence. I widen my stance, tighten my grip around my baton, and lower the shield of my helmet.

Game on.

I look up just in time to see an object hurled by a cowardly protester. A half-eaten burrito lands in front of my feet. Looks like a supreme from Muchas Gracias. What a waste.

There is a moment of uneasy silence. Lights emitting from the high-intensity stage lamps appear to fade, casting ghostly shadows on the walls. Suddenly hundreds of projectiles (rocks, bottles, mortars) are launched from the crowd. This air assault of objects in flight appear to hover in the sky and temporarily eclipse the surrounding lights.

I realize that the burrito was a sacrifice to ascertain distance and trajectory.

Genius. I would not have sacrificed my burrito. For the first time, I realize I have underestimated the resolve of these hooligans. Now we stand exposed to hundreds of projectiles descending upon us like a tropical rain.

The sound of bottles breaking and rocks clashing with our helmets emboldens the crowd as they push harder on the fence. Any second now the fence is going to crumble, like Nancy Kerrigan's knees, under the exorbitant weight of the angry crowd. The Incident Commander (IC) tells us to retreat farther away from the fence as the sound truck gives multiple verbal dispersals and "use of force" warnings.

The crowd ignores all warnings and continues to throw projectiles and mortars over the fence line. The sound of exploding projectiles triggers a distant memory, and for a brief moment I think I'm back in the streets of Baghdad. I suppress those bitter memories as I anxiously await the "unlawful assembly" announcement to be made. This announcement gives those of us in uniforms the green light to take lawful yet controlled violent action against the violent crowd.

My prayers are soon answered as the sound truck makes the announcement: "This is an unlawful assembly. Leave now or you will be subject to riot control munitions or use of force."

The crowd responds with a thunderous "boo" and sends another wave of projectiles into the air. A green laser crosses my vision, and I quickly close my eyes to protect them, as I recall the eye damage sustained by a JetBlue pilot after two laser beams were shone into his inbound plane.

For sixteen days straight now, this cowardly individual has been lurking behind the crowd targeting his laser at police officers. His day of judgment will come. The universe will balance itself, and the hand of karma will reach through the veil and grab him by the throat. We will meet soon, my friend.

Multiple riot control teams move in from the north and send flash bangs and smoke toward the crowd. A few days ago a U.S. district judge, Marco A. Hernandez, backed up Mayor Wheeler's restriction on the use of CS gas, a type of tear gas, by the police force. The judge concluded that protesters were "engaged only in peaceful non-destructive protest." I think Apple and other businesses in downtown Portland, after being vandalized and looted by these "peaceful" protesters, may have had a few comments to voice about that. To date, all of these businesses remain boarded as protesters continue to ravage the downtown Portland area.[3]

Smoke quickly envelops the crowd as they disperse in groups headed south and west, away from the fence line. The sound truck continues to give the warning of dispersal as Riot Response Teams push the crowd out of Chapman Park.

Vehicles supplying the crowd with projectiles circle the block and throw explosive devices and fireworks toward officers before speeding away. The fence line and Chapman Park are cleared within minutes, and the Mobile Field Force (MFF) jumps into action.

By the time the park is cleared, I join the rest of my team (three marked patrol cars with four officers per car) just outside the wire in order to make contact with those who are refusing to leave, search for criminal activity, and make arrests.

For countless nights we have engaged with members of the domestic terrorist group, Antifa and BLM, many of whom have been armed with metal pipes, knives, blunt objects, and handguns. Each evening they become more organized, more prepared, and more hostile. Sounds of flash bangs and improvised explosive devices echo through the streets, rattling the remaining windows that have not yet been busted out. Transients are forced to scurry along, moving from one sleeping corner to another. One such individual yells, "Shut the fuck up, I'm trying to sleep," as he scuttles to the next corner, hoping to find a quiet place to lay his head.

Not tonight, my friend, nor for many nights to come.

Members of both BLM and Antifa run through the smoke-filled streets setting pallets, dumpsters, and buildings ablaze. I attempt to see these vile acts through the eyes of those who believe this to be a peaceful protest. However, common sense, deductive reasoning, and logic leave me shaking my head in disbelief.

I pull my gloves tighter around my fists, check the strap on my helmet, and prepare myself to jump out of the squad car to face chaos and what most would call terror.

Mobile Field Force, let's do what we do best.

CHAPTER 6

OPERATION SNATCH AND GRAB

It is 10:30 in the evening, and I'm nursing my fifth cup of coffee.

I'm not sure anymore what day we're on of the chaos and civil unrest triggered by the death of George Floyd two time zones away.

My team and I are staged in a dark parking lot on the corner of Thirteenth and SW Main. For the last two hours we have circled the city in search of vehicles carrying items that could be used as barricades or as fuel to start fires. Many downtown businesses have been set ablaze these last two weeks, leaving Portland in ruins. Antifa and other anti-fascism groups have descended upon our city like a plague of locusts devouring fruits of commerce and peace.

I look around at my team and see officers exhausted beyond measure, men and women with abrasions and bruises from previous nights of battle. I remove my right glove to inspect a cut on my knuckle. It's starting to itch. It must be healing.

Two nights ago while on patrol, we stumbled upon a group of "protesters" attempting to loot a business. When we rounded the corner, these cowards ran like cockroaches darting into dark alleys, scared to face the light of justice they deserve. I bolted out of my squad car in pursuit of a dark-clothed male running westbound away from the main group of criminals he was with. Fueled by adrenaline and a "tired of this shit" frame of mind, I reached maximum velocity within a fraction of a second and quickly closed the gap on what he probably thought was enough distance to make his escape.

I was a split second from giving the weakling a good old-fashioned, hard-hitting, Ray Lewis–type tackle.

Suddenly, I noticed another officer nearby struggling to control two combative subjects, one of whom was armed with a metal pipe. The armed subject had managed to break free and was midswing with his weapon when I quickly altered my direction of travel, went airborne, and delivered a cold shoulder to his midriff.

The impact lifted him off his feet and sent him to the ground gasping for air. Unbeknownst to him, the ground is my comfort zone. Ten-plus years of getting my ass handed to me during training has saved me during countless physical altercations with gangsters, drug dealers, and other nefarious characters.

The man-made futile attempts to escape, but he was no match for the sheer power and ferocity (mine) that fell upon him.

Okay, I'm boasting a little. And exaggerating.

Besides, the half can of pepper spray my sergeant unloaded on his face may have also played a role in helping calm the man down a bit.

Truth be told, the man surprised me with his strength, speed, and recovery from the tackle. After handcuffing the subject, I looked at my right hand and noticed I was bleeding through my glove. I bandaged the abrasion and continued to make additional arrests before the night came to an end.

That was two nights ago.

What tonight will bring remains to be seen.

In the dark parking lot, I get out of the vehicle to look for a place to relieve myself when Incident Command breaks radio silence.

"I need a free Mobile Field Force to come back to the Justice Center for a special mission," a voice crackles over the airwaves.

My sergeant, Samson, responds to the call, accepting the task at hand. He then tells everyone to load up into the vehicles.

I quickly zip up my pants and run to the car, feeling dribbling down the side of my leg. By the time I get to the car, I see a wet spot on my pants the size of my fist. I'm about to curse out loud when I realize that will only draw further unwanted attention from my team.

We arrive at the controlled southern entrance of the heavily fortified Justice Center and make our way toward the front of the building as Samson gets "the call."

I jump out of the squad car and begin to off-load gear from my body. I suspect the mission will require speed and agility. Yesterday a member of Antifa climbed over the fence line and walked unchallenged for fifteen minutes inciting the crowed on the other side. A team of officers were sent to apprehend the subject, but miraculously he was able to outrun the gear-heavy officers and awkwardly throw his nonathletic body over the fence unscathed. The crowd cheered and cele-brated as if Alexander the Great had returned from his mul-tination conquest.

Samson hangs up the phone and tells us to gather around him.

"Okay, sounds like we have another guy over the fence," Samson says, "and he is refusing to return to the other side. He may or may not be same guy from yesterday. The plan is to use the sound truck that's on the north side to distract the crowd and we come in from the south side. We take two vehicles and drive to where he is at, grab him, and bring him back here. We need to get this guy. Who are my runners?"

I quickly raise my hand, and before Samson can give his approval, I begin to off-load more gear from my vest and waist-band. I need to be as light as possible. This time he will not get away, nor will the crowd be celebrating a "hero's return."

Samson gives another order to load up.

We load back into our vehicles and slowly drive west-bound on the south side of the Justice Center. In order to conceal our approach, we ask Incident Command to dim the floodlights on the south side of the Justice Center. I am in the backseat of the patrol car holding the door slightly open as we make our way to the corner of SW Third and Madison.

I hear the sound truck give dispersal warnings to the defiant crowd—a crowd oblivious to the cataclysm that is just around the corner, embodied by two police cars loaded with seven battle-ready officers on a mission to deliver the simple message that we have had enough. We have had enough of the racist and discriminatory remarks fueled by ignorance and insatiable hate toward men and women of law enforcement.

Today, at least one will feel the wrath from this monster they have slowly created. The specialized skills, training, and knowledge we possess have been lying in wait over the last few years, only to be roused by the chaos and evil our city is experiencing at the hands of unlawful hate groups. Now, like a great storm brewing in the distance, they are culminating in a very focused way and will rain down on these unsuspecting domestic terrorists in such a manner they cannot begin to fathom.

We round the corner of Third and Madison, and I spot the target, a masked male wearing jeans and a white T-shirt. He is standing on a cement barricade leading the crowd into a senseless "ACAB" chant.

The crowd, like a bunch of mindless mooing cows, respond with "All Cops Are Bastards!"

I take a few deep breaths in rapid succession, flooding my lungs with oxygen. Red blood cells in my body rush to intercept oxygen in the capillaries of my lungs, saturating my muscles and prepping them for the punishment that is about to be unleashed.

I tell Samson to "step on the gas" as the masked subject turns his attention toward our speeding patrol car.

He goes into a state of panic and reaches for the fence to make his escape.

The crowd erupts, and a few begin to climb the other side in an attempt to pull their hero back to safety. The subject is wearing a shirt that is too big for his frame, and fabric snags a jagged edge of the fence. A jagged edge of the fence that was previously cut by a protestor a few days ago before being struck by a 40-millimeter, less lethal round.

I tell Samson to anchor the patrol vehicle, and like a coiled snake I explode out of the car before Samson has applied the brakes. Newton's first law of motion quickly takes over and throws me slightly off balance. I apply the necessary amount of opposing force to break free from Newton's grasp.

Exposed wire prevents our suspect from reaching the top of the fence, and he jumps down on the top of the cement barrier next to the fence line.

I launch my body into the air, colliding with the subject as he jumps off the barrier.

The force of the midair collision sends us both airborne approximately four feet off the ground.

We land alongside the next cement barrier as the strap on my helmet breaks from the impact. My helmet ejects off my head and rolls somewhere a few feet away.

Immediately, the crowd retaliates by launching bottles, rocks, and half-eaten burritos toward my team and our vehicles.

A few of my team members surround me and form a human shield blocking the onslaught of projectiles thrown from the cowards in the crowd. As I struggle to handcuff their fallen "hero," I can hear the sound of bottles breaking and rocks colliding with helmets, glass, and metal.

Anytime now I am going to catch a bottle or a rock to the head.

We need to move fast.

No time to handcuff this fool.

I jump to my feet and pull our soon-to-be-in-custody suspect to his feet. Another officer and I push him ahead of us as we run to the back of the second patrol car. Without hesitation I hurl our subject in the back of the squad car and jump in as we continue to get pelted with rocks and bottles.

I am in the process of closing my door when an improvised explosive device (IED) explodes about a foot from my door. Showers of sparks and smoke envelop my vehicle. Traveling faster than the speed of sound, the blast wave radiates in all directions and is quickly followed by a negative pressure wave. Some of the blast waves are deflected by the Justice Center which is east of us, instantly magnifying the impact of the blast.

The world around me goes silent as I struggle to hear my own voice over the high-pitched ringing inside my ears.

"Get us the hell out of here!" I yell.

My ears are ringing as I force the face of our man in custody toward the hard seat and warn him not to move.

Normally I would handcuff my custody before he or she sits in the backseat of my patrol car, but desperate times call for desperate measures. Just as expected, the crowd's proclaimed hero offers no resistance in the backseat and shakes like a newborn puppy.

We reach the front of the Justice Center within seconds, and I get out with my frightened custody. I quickly zip-tie his hands behind his back and tell him he is under arrest for trespassing and other charges.

I don't mention that the charges against him are likely to be dropped by Multnomah County District Attorney-Elect Mike Schmidt who recently told The Oregonian and Oregon Live that he will "look really hard" at the types of cases he is going to prosecute. In addition, Schmidt boldly stated, "I am considering dropping charges against non-violent protestors."[4]

The people who elected this overzealous DA will be the first to criticize law enforcement when criminals roam free in the streets of Portland.

My ears still ringing, I walk my custody inside the Justice Center knowing he will be set free before the end of my shift. Shortly after, he will reunite with his domestic terrorist group and take part in multiple criminal activities, preying on the people who want to defund the police.

Welcome to Portland, no longer a city of roses but of chaos and despair.

Chapter 7

GUN VIOLENCE REDUCTION TEAM (GVRT)

July 2020

It is the height of the summer in July 2020, and our battle with Antifa and the Black Lives Matter (BLM) rages as they continue to destroy and loot businesses across the city of Portland.

Liberal politicians continue to label the carnage as "peaceful" protests, despite the fact that these "peaceful" protests have resulted in significant injuries among the ranks and file of the Portland Police Bureau and other officers and deputies from other agencies.

The rioting has been going nonstop since May 29, 2020, and every day Antifa and BLM become more organized and more violent toward police officers and civilians refusing to conform to their dangerous ideology. They preach about social injustice and racial inequality, yet they continue to destroy black-owned businesses in Portland and in cities across the

United States. They have terrorized neighborhoods all over the United States demanding city politicians defund police agencies without consideration of the disastrous outcome of a city without law and order.

Members of BLM even marched to a predominately white neighborhoods in Seattle and Portland demanding white residents to give up their homes. Homes they claimed belong to them. One man was heard yelling, "Do you know that before your white ass came here, this was all black people?"[5] *White ass*, I'm sure if that script was flipped there would be a full court press with every liberal media outlet in the United States.

As the summer heat continues to rise, so do calls for service. Priority calls, including "shots fired," are put on hold as we deal with multiple shootings all over the city of Portland. Most of the calls will hold until the following day when the next shift comes in. Lower-priority calls will hold for over twenty-four hours, when most will be canceled by a supervisor, followed by a phone call explaining to the caller why police cannot respond to their call for service.

Between multiple shootings a day and the nightly riots in Portland, resources are stretched thin. Officers are beginning to feel the effects of prolonged duty hours, physical exertion, lack of sleep, and adrenaline fatigue from going from call to call defending the city against the violent extremist groups known as Antifa and Black Lives Matter.

Yet in the city of Portland, Commissioner Jo Ann Hardesty has been relentless in her pursuit of defunding the Portland Police Bureau.

This week I have responded to eight shootings and conducted CPR on two victims with multiple gunshot wounds. Neither of those victims survived. I remember the days where we would find maybe one or two casings inside the crime scene—now we are finding thirty, forty, sometimes over fifty casings. The streets of Portland have become a war zone for rival gangs gleefully aware of the decline in proactive policing due to the overwhelming demands placed on police by the nightly destruction perpetrated by Antifa and BLM.

Morale is at its lowest, we are overridden with burgeoning crime, and Antifa and BLM terrorist groups are more organized and violent than ever.

And Portland law enforcement—and the city we serve—was just dealt a devastating blow.

For the past year, Commissioner Jo Ann Hardesty has been campaigning to dismantle the Gun Violence Reduction Team (GVRT) as a part of defunding the Portland Police Bureau.

On June 9, 2020, Mayor Ted Wheeler surrenders to Jo Ann Hardesty's desire and dismantles the GVRT. He claims it is the right step toward police reform.

They are both dead wrong.

GVRT—originally named the Gang Enforcement Team (GET)—was a specialized unit of highly trained officers who responded to shooting calls inside the city. They processed crime scenes—including diagramming, conducting interviews, canvassing, and executing door-to-door follow-ups—with a level of detail that's difficult to replicate as a patrol officer due to the sheer number of calls we respond to every day.

Members of GVRT also developed relationships within the community—often with families of gang members. They were keenly aware of the key players—and especially repeat shooters—within active gangs.

GVRT officers were also familiar with the vehicles associated with gang members and places they frequented. I've been at many crime scenes when GVRT offers arrived, looked at surveillance footage, and were able to identify the shooter within seconds. As you can imagine, this saves precious time and provides everyone the ability to disseminate critical information rapidly to other officers and surrounding agencies, which translates into more expedient arrests, preventing additional shootings that would have resulted from rival gangs taking revenge.

Through intel gathering and case follow-ups, GVRT officers often developed probable cause to stop vehicles belonging to criminals on their way to conduct a drive-by shooting or an execution-style homicide.

These tactics fall under what we know today as proactive policing, a concept that is aggressively opposed by Democrat-led cities across America.

But here's why it's so damn important: in order to combat crime and the fear of crime, a proactive approach must be the cornerstone of any plan. You cannot lie and wait for the next shooting to take place; you must prioritize intelligence gathering, develop cooperative relationships with community members, and allow community leaders (not to be confused with city politicians) to have a platform in the fight against crime.

Patrol officers can't replicate the work of GVRT.

Those of us on patrol have noticed the immediate consequence of the vacuum left by the Gun Violence Reduction Team.

Since Hardesty, Antifa, and BLM dismantled GVRT with their continued drumbeat of defund the police, the responsibility of processing crime scenes, which used to be handled by GVRT, has shifted to responding patrol officers. After every shooting, multiple officers are tied up at the crime scene for hours and sometimes for their entire shifts. Sometimes not a single police officer is available to respond to subsequent shootings or active burglaries or other crimes. Officers from different precincts or agencies are often requested to assist in order to manage priority calls that never seem to stop coming.

And it doesn't take a scientist or a case study to tell you that if you remove police officers off the street, especially those who specialize in the reduction of gun violence, crime will spread like herpes at a Woodstock concert.

And, indeed, homicides and drive-by shootings have risen faster than the popularity of boy bands in the mid 1990s. I had a few albums myself.

Here is my prediction: the careless removal of our Gun Violence Reduction Team will continue to have dismal consequences for a city that's already under attack by violent extremists like Antifa and BLM.

Gangs giddy over the collapse of the Gun Violence Reduction Team will continue to come out of the shadows to lay siege against peace and order.

Drug and sex trafficking will continue to rise as criminals require more income to acquire additional weapons and recruitment of others.

Bodies will continue to pile up on the streets of Portland, and the city will continue to see the highest number of homicides it has ever seen.

And every year these tragic records will continue to be broken until city politicians recognize their grave error in judgment and actually place the needs of its citizens above their own.

These are the consequences that city council members have not stopped to consider. Their decision to end the GVRT was based on emotions and false narratives, made without the benefit of critical thinking and analysis.

To Jo Ann Hardesty, the removal of GVRT provided a few drops of water for her insatiable thirst for power and her quest to completely defund the entire Portland Police Bureau. For the citizens of Portland, these defunding actions will have a long-lasting impact on the community of color as they continue to see their sons and daughters lie on the streets in pools of blood.

Politicians love to preach about community policing, but the truth is community policing cannot exist without proactive policing. Proactive policing utilized by GVRT and other officers allows for community engagement that significantly lessens or prevents the occurrence of crime. In other words, tragic events are avoided or decreased when hardworking police officers who truly care about people—black or white—are allowed to conduct proactive policing.

In the last few months, we officers on patrol have done little to zero community policing. And if we continue down the ill-chosen path of being a reactive organization, this isn't going to change.

Patrol officers will never have the time or resources to engage in the kind of focused, proactive community policing provided by Portland's GVRT. Even now, the amount of resources, time, and personnel utilized in dealing with the multiple shootings throughout Portland is unsustainable.

You want to take the wind out of an officer's sail who is proactive and hungry for crime fighting? Tell him or her that he or she cannot conduct a traffic or subject stop. In the event that an officer stops a subject who happens to be a person of color, there is now that fear of being labeled a racist.

Unfortunately, this is the world that liberals have created for law enforcement officers around the United States. I have had personal conversations with white officers whom I have heard say, "I won't stop a black person; I don't want to be called a racist." This is a disheartening reality that will require a mass removal of divisive liberal politicians and media to reverse the damages they have inflicted on communities across the United States and on the psyche of many officers who were insistently labeled as racist. The next election cannot come fast enough.

One can only hope that the people of Portland will hold these politicians accountable for their actions.

CHAPTER 8

THE SIEGE OF EAST PRECINCT

August 2020

For more than seventy days, we have watched Antifa, BLM, and other domestic terrorist groups lay siege to multiple critical infrastructure facilities in the city of Portland.

Businesses across Portland remain closed and boarded for the unforeseeable future. Night after night, rioters have set fires in the middle of the streets while looting businesses that are already struggling to survive.

We arrest perpetrators for arson, assault, criminal mischief, disorderly conduct, theft, interfering with a police officer, and rioting. The district attorney of Portland then refuses to prosecute these arrests.

People with logic and common sense cannot understand why these charges are dropped.

And just when you think that the level of lunacy and ignorance can't get any worse, Portland Commissioner Jo

Ann Hardesty states, "I want people to know that I do not believe there's any protesters in Portland that are setting fires, that are creating crisis. I absolutely believe it's police action, and they're sending saboteurs and provocateurs into peaceful crowds so they justify their inhumane treatment of people who are standing up for their rights."[6]

Of course, Hardesty is unable to provide any shred of tangible evidence to support her idiotic statement. I've often pondered how a person in her position could possess so much hatred toward law enforcement. She frequently speaks of white supremacy or racism but offers no evidence of her accusations. She refuses to acknowledge that violent gangsters exist in the city of Portland despite the fact that an overwhelming majority of them self-identify as gangsters. They flaunt their color designation and tattoos, and their markings can be seen throughout the city. Even with all the irrefutable evidence, Jo Ann Hardesty refuses to believe gangs exist in Portland.

For many days the focus of attacks and riots has been directed at the core downtown area. Every police precinct has been vandalized or set on fire, with the exception of East Precinct, my home.

Repeatedly, our command team has assured us, "They will not touch East Precinct, you can bet on that." We were told that plans had been set in place to protect East Precinct.

On August 5, 2020, I sit in roll call drinking my whey protein shake and scrolling through the email on my cell phone. My glutes and quads are still shaking from the squats and lunges I completed moments earlier. The captain, lieutenant, and several sergeants walk into the room, indicating that roll call is about to start.

One sergeant takes a deep breath and says, "Well, our intel says that they are coming to East Precinct tonight."

I swallow the last of my muscle builder, then start thumbing a text to a few of my cop buddies. A few of these officers are taking a much-needed first day off in weeks; others are home with serious injuries sustained during the riots.

I rub my left elbow, still feeling some pain from an injury I received weeks ago. This injury was worth getting, as I apprehended a terrorist that day. I made a grown man realize he still had a lot of growing left to do and just how insignificant his actions were in this universe.

We knew this was coming. It was just a matter of time. We've been psychologically ready for weeks, and the waiting has felt excruciating. Now it's game time.

I text the missing officers: Y'ALL PICKED THE WRONG TIME TO BE SITTING ON YOUR COUCH EATING DONUTS AND WATCHING RERUNS OF COPS. THESE TERRORISTS ARE COMING TO EAST PRECINCT.

The sergeants tell us to go out and take calls as normal. They tell us that when the protesters arrive at East Precinct, we will be recalled, and the plan of action will be initiated. The plan is to barricade all avenues of entry to the precinct and stop these terrorists before they can do damage to the precinct.

At around 1900 hours, we get the call to return to East Precinct. I turn on my lights and sirens and speed toward East Precinct. Looking left and right at streets paralleling mine, I see other police cars racing toward the precinct too.

We arrive and park our patrol cars on the upper level of the parking garage.

I go to my trunk and grab my helmet and gas mask, then run downstairs to the roll call room and wait for other officers to show. After a few minutes there are fourteen officers inside the precinct, leaving only two police cars (two officers per car) on the streets to cover all of East Portland's emergency calls. I put my gloves on and prepare myself for battle.

A supervisor is standing at the front of the room and talking.

He tells us to stay inside the building and hunker down.

I look around at other officers to see if I'm the only one confused about the change of plan. Then I ask the question that I'm sure everyone was thinking: "How are we supposed to protect the precinct from the inside? What happened to the plan that was put in place weeks ago?"

The supervisor clears his throat. "Incident Command has overridden that plan, and you are now to stay inside the precinct."

I shake my head in disbelief.

I think back on the four years I spent as a company commander in the army, making command decisions on the ground. When I was given a mission by higher authorities, as the commander of the unit I was able to make decisions as to how that mission was to be executed. I cannot imagine being given a mission and not being given the authority to decide how to execute that mission.

I feel pity for the precinct commander, captain, lieutenant, and sergeants. I look around at my leadership and see experienced officers, capable of making intelligent decisions. Yet their authority is being neutered by an Incident Command team ten miles away, making decisions based on live-feed videos and other means of intelligence gathering.

This structure of command and control will never give rise to leaders capable of decisive action in an operational environment and needs to be revised.

A sergeant instructs a few of us to cover rooftop corners and designates a team to protect the entrance to the garage.

I run to my marked patrol car to get my Polarion lights and my binoculars. Polarion searchlights have been invaluable against rioters who are flashing bright lights and lasers into police officers' eyes. You should see the look on rioters' faces when they are hit by 4,800 lumens of a high-intensity discharge (HID) lamp. Lines suddenly appear on their foreheads as the muscles around their eyes involuntarily contract from the intensity of the light. One time I heard someone from the crowd yell, "Fuck, I can't see, what the fuck is that?" The person quickly turned and groped his way blindly to the back of the crowd.

I made the mistake once of testing the Polarion in front of the mirror, and it took me about thirty seconds to fully regain my vision.

I walk to the outlet on the north side of the rooftop and plug in both Polarion lights. When used on high setting, these lights will last for about an hour on a continuous run. Intermittent use of the light usually prolongs the battery life to about two and half hours.

Assigned as roving security, I position myself on the east wall of the rooftop. I look east and scan the parking lot directly across the precinct. I can hear BLM and Antifa stroking each other with their "All cops are bastards" chant from somewhere nearby.

In my earpiece, the pilot of one of two surveillance planes announces that a group of about 250 are gathered at the football field across the precinct, just shy of my field of view. Looking down, I see an unusual amount of vehicular traffic in front of the precinct. A white Ford Ranger drives by, and I see two red gas cans on the bed of the truck. I take out my binoculars to get the license plate number on the vehicle and a description of the driver. This is definitely a supply vehicle.

Supply vehicles play an integral role for rioters, providing fireworks, projectiles, accelerants, pepper spray, barricades, and other items to aid with nefarious activities.

I get on the radio and report what I see to Incident Command.

I continue scanning the parking lot with my binoculars and see a white male putting on body armor. After checking the fit and the straps on his armor, the subject reaches for a black sweatshirt and puts it on over his body armor. He is now dressed completely in black. I place the camera of my iPhone next to one of the eye cups of my binoculars and take a close-up photo of the subject, as I am sure he will commit some type of crime later on in the evening and I will then have a photo of him without his mask.

The noise of passing cars is quickly interrupted by the sound of a beating drum. Looking toward the direction of the football field, I see a line of protesters marching toward the precinct. Each one is dressed in black with helmets, body armor, and shields.

Their appearance belies the claims of many city leaders that this is a "peaceful protest."

The sound of the drum gets louder as they march closer to the front of the precinct. The drummer is clearly visible now. I recognize the drummer—a man dressed as a woman—as someone I have arrested numerous times for disorderly conduct and interfering with a police officer. Each time I've arrested him, he's been wearing his signature attire of Skirt No Panties (SNP), which I've had the displeasure of discovering to be true while he fought the arrest, flailing around like a fish out of water.

A group of about three hundred is now gathered in front of East Precinct, chanting "ACAB." It doesn't take long for the spotlights to come out, and within seconds I'm blinded by four or five spotlights from the crowd.

I reach for my Polarion.

Suddenly, over the radio I hear someone from Incident Command say, "Officers on the rooftop, step back from the edge. The crowd is reacting to your presence."

I walk away from the ledge, shaking my head in disbelief. The officer next to me follows suit.

"This defeats the purpose of having an overwatch," I say to him. "How are we to observe and report if we can't fucking see the threat? Now we are completely fucking blind because everyone else is inside the building and security cameras can only see a small part of the crowd."

Furious with Incident Command, I grab my helmet and walk inside the precinct.

I walk to the lower part of the secured garage and check with other officers. They, too, are shaking their heads and wondering why we are not outside defending our precinct.

A few minutes pass and the sergeant calls me to the main lobby of the precinct. I hear on the radio that a few members of the crowd are now throwing boulders and concrete blocks at the glass doors and windows of the precinct.

I enter the main lobby that leads to the front doors and see the captain, sergeant, and five other officers. On the other side of the bulletproof glass is a mob of approximately three hundred members of Antifa and Black Lives Matter. One black male is pressed up against the glass screaming at the top of his lungs, "Fuck you! You ain't shit without that badge. I would beat your ass in a fight. Come out here without your gun and badge, and I will beat the shit of you!"

I stare directly into this man's eyes and envision about a hundred different ways I could dismantle him.

He continues to spew his rhetoric and his dream of "beating my ass" while pressing both middle fingers on the glass. He then turns around, drops his saggy pants, and presses his bare ass on the glass. Then, pulling up his pants, he picks up a boulder-size rock and repeatedly throws it at the door and window.

The sergeant tells Incident Command, "We are now taking large-size rocks to the front door and windows of the precinct."

Incident Command responds, "We are not there yet, do not engage."

The Riot Response Team (RRT) and State Patrol are staged just a few blocks away awaiting command from IMT (Incident Management Team) to engage the crowd. I can hear the sound truck give admonishments to the crowd, telling them to stop all criminal activity or be subjected to use of force.

At that moment, another black male walks up to the windows north of the doorway and holds up a dirty white sock just below his chin. The way the sock sways back and forth I can tell it's filled with something. The terrorist then grabs the bottom of the sock and turns it upside down and empties the content into his gloved hand.

After filling his hand full of feces, he smears it all over the window at eye level. He continues to paint the entire window with feces and throws the sock and feces-covered gloves against the double doors. The sock sticks for a brief moment before slowly sliding toward the ground, leaving a brown streak that reminds me what my underwear looks like after ten hours on the front line of battle.

I look at the streaks on the window and feel an uncontrollable spasm in my stomach. I look away for a brief moment in an attempt to keep the contents inside my stomach from rising to my throat. Anger supersedes the nausea, and I direct my attention toward the front doors. The front doors now have visible cracks that look like a spider web. Two subjects continue to throw boulders toward the front doors while others stack wood and other flammable material against the building.

Out of nowhere a ladder slams against the top portion of the entryway, and a white male begins to climb to the top of the ladder. Another subject hands him a ball-peen hammer, and he begins to hammer on the glass above the doorway.

I grab a large can (party can) of pepper spray in each hand, and I widen my stance. I look at the two 40-millimeter operators, and I give them a nod. This is where we will make our stand. The terrorists will not get past the lobby.

The window above the doorway is now beginning to crack from the force of the hammer. The protester wielding the hammer is relentless in his attempt to break the glass, as beads of sweat begin to form on his forehead.

An officer next to me records the man's action with his cell phone, and protesters immediately react by covering the windows with cardboard to block the officer from collecting evidence. I hear the sounds of metal scraping the surface of the concrete sidewalk as additional plywood is stacked against the front door of the precinct.

A large metal garbage can is now pressed against the doorway and within seconds the contents inside the garbage can are set on fire. A protester sets a two-by-four inside the flaming garbage can and leans it against the precinct doors. The wood must have marinated in some type of an accelerant because the flame quickly rises to the top of the two-by-four and is now licking the side of the building.

A protester walks up to the front entrance and slides another two-by-four in the handles of the double doors.

"Burn, mother fuckers!" he yells as he takes a few steps back away from the fire.

The front doors are now completely barricaded which leaves us only two other exits if the building catches on fire.

The sergeant gets on the radio and tells the Incident Commander. "We now have a fire outside the front doors, and flames are going up the side of the building. A two-by-four is wedged in the handle of the doors, so we are completely barricaded. The glass doors and windows are beginning to crack from all the rocks. Eventually they will break through, or the building will catch on fire."

"We are not there yet," the Incident Commander says. "Sound truck, continue giving the announcement of dispersal and use-of-force warning."

I look at my sergeant and say, "What the fuck does he mean we are not there yet? We have homes attached to this building, and we have civilians inside this precinct."

My feelings of anger turn to rage as I look around and see the frustration on the faces of other officers around me.

Over the radio, I hear the voice of a seasoned officer on the rooftop who has forgotten more about police work than some members of Incident Management Team (IMT) will ever see.

"I have a hose and I have water," he tells Incident Command. "I can at least put the fire out. I can also pepper spray the people who are adding wood to the fire."

Incident Command rejects the offer and tells the sound truck to continue with dispersal admonishments and warnings.

Unfortunately, no actions can be taken until the Incident Commander declares an "unlawful assembly" or a "riot."

Lincoln 1, the Riot Response Team leader, tells Incident Command, "I think we have enough to declare a riot." I hear the frustration in his voice.

As the flames double in size, the Incident Commander debates with the sound truck operators about a recent ruling from a federal judge. He tells the sound truck to use the word "tear gas" instead of "CS gas" in order to be in compliance with the judge's ruling.

The level of frustration inside the lobby has now risen to the point where all officers are ready to execute independent action. Rioters continue to attack the windows and doors with boulders and chunks of broken concrete.

The integrity of the glass is severely compromised as the spiderweb cracks grow longer and connect with others like it.

The man on top of the ladder continues his assault on the upper glass, and the sound of each impact now echoes inside the lobby.

We stack tables and chairs in front of the long windows and doors to slow down the mob if they break through the glass.

I prepare myself the best way I know how and run scenarios inside my head. I can probably pepper spray at least ten to twelve rioters with each party can of pepper spray before running out. After that it's hand-to-hand combat. Maybe I should set aside the cans of pepper spray and go straight to pound town.

My thoughts are interrupted by the sounds of multiple explosions followed by showers of sparks. Within seconds the entire front area of East Precinct is covered with tear gas and smoke.

The cavalry has arrived.

Officers from the RRT begin to materialize like ghosts floating through a thick fog over a graveyard. The horde is in a state of panic as they scramble north on SE 106th toward Stark. A few unfortunate rioters are tackled on the streets and quickly zip-tied and searched for weapons.

A State Patrol officer assigned to the RRT pulls the six-foot two-by-four that is wedged inside the door handles and throws it to the ground. We quickly open the doors and pick up the rocks, broken pieces of concrete, and the two by four and pull them inside the lobby.

An officer dressed in riot gear grabs me by the arm. "Hey," he says, "I need someone to get my patrol car and drive it inside the parking garage before these idiots vandalize it."

I grab another officer, and we run outside toward the patrol car. By the time I take my second step, I realize my mistake. I'm not wearing my gas mask, and it's too late to put it on now.

The gas hits my lungs like razor-sharp needles, and instantly I'm coughing uncontrollably, and my eyes and face are on fire like I just washed my face in habanero hot sauce.

Through the thick fog of gas, I search for the door handle of the driver-side door and find it locked. I reach inside my pocket in search of my keys as I continue to cough and fight the uncontrollable contractions of the muscles around my eyes.

My eyes are now gushing with tears as I fight to keep them open to see the keyhole on the driver-side door. I manage to unlock the vehicle and reach inside to unlock the passenger door for my partner. I start the engine and tell my partner to block the air from the outside and circulate the air inside the vehicle. We scramble to put our masks on inside the protection of the vehicle and quickly clear the air inside the mask.

"Man," I say to my partner, "you're gonna have to help me back up because I can't see anything. I can't keep my eyes open."

My partner coughs uncontrollably. Between the coughs, I think I hear, "Yeah, man, I can't see either, but I got you."

I slowly back the patrol car twenty-five yards, through the smoke and tear gas covering the entire street in front of the precinct. My vision is severely compromised, my face is on fire, and my lungs continue to expel the remnants of the tear gas I swallowed outside the car. We manage to find the front door of the garage and pull the vehicle inside.

I bolt out of the vehicle and quickly remove my mask. I take my first breath of fresh air and reel in the mucus dragging toward the ground from my nose. I sever the mucus with my fingers by pinching my nose and wiping my slimy fingers on my pants. No time for a tissue.

We run back to the main lobby and assess the damage to the front door. The fire is now extinguished, but the glass and concrete are covered in white powder (sodium bicarbonate) from the fire extinguisher.

We pick up all the remaining rocks and projectiles thrown at the precinct and carry them inside the lobby. The Riot Response Team (RRT) continues to disperse the crowd and makes multiple arrests on SE 106th just south of Stark. The crowd is pushed all the way to Stark, and then they disperse east and west on Stark. Incident Command tells the Mobile Field Force to drive around with lights and sirens and continue to push the crowd away from the precinct.

My team is tasked with guarding the precinct and blocking the entrance to SE 106th from Stark. It's a maneuver that was set in place days prior to the attack but delayed when Incident Command thought it was more appropriate to hide inside the precinct and watch rioters set fire to an occupied building.

I can tell everyone is eager to step outside the precinct as we put on our gear and form a line on the north entrance of the precinct.

Incident Command gives us the green light to exit, and we rush toward the front of the precinct. The street in front of the precinct, SE 106th, is littered with gas and smoke canisters and items dropped by the rioters running from RRT. We block SE 106th from vehicular and pedestrian traffic and form a security bubble around the precinct.

We play cat and mouse with the rioters for the next two hours and make additional arrests, including the arrest of an armed Antifa member posing as a member of the press.

For the past seventy plus days we have arrested protesters armed with pistols, brass knuckles, baseball bats, knives, and other devious homemade weapons. Many claim to be residents of Oregon, screaming, "We pay your taxes! You work for us!" Yet most are felons and not residents of Oregon. These individuals are professional rioters who are funded by millionaires who do not believe in law and order or government.

The night ends, not with a celebration of victory, but with feelings of sadness, anger, and betrayal.

This evening we watched Antifa and BLM lay siege to our home uncontested. Each day they are emboldened by the inaction and ineffectiveness of Incident Command and city leadership. The district attorney's refusal to prosecute has ignited an unprecedented level of violence toward law enforcement officers and citizens who support law and order.

Portland has become a modern-day Sodom or Gomorrah, a city that embodies the worst of human life and lawlessness.

Someday I will leave this morally corrupt city, and just like Lot I will not turn back.

CHAPTER 9

CONCRETE JUSTICE

August 31, 2020

Today is Mayor Ted Wheeler's birthday—and the ninety-sixth day of nonstop rioting and chaos.

As usual, the internet is full of chatter and videos from previous nights of lawlessness, pandemonium, and chaos in Portland, which continues to dominate the airtime of multiple media platforms.

Today Antifa and Black Lives Matter are organizing a "birthday party" for Teddy, a party he undoubtedly will not attend. This is because the people Mayor Ted Wheeler is trying to protect and pacify are revolting against him. According to internet chatter, Antifa and BLM are displeased with how Ted is addressing police reform. For the past ninety-six days, Antifa and BLM have strongly voiced their demand to completely abolish the Portland Police Bureau. Their demands can be clearly seen in the many signs they have paraded night after night of violent demonstrations: "Defund the police" or "No racist police."

I recall a conversation with an Asian female on day 8 of the riots. She approached the fence that protects the Justice Center and boldly stated, "Brother, my Asian brother, aren't you ashamed of what you are doing? Take off your uniform and join us on this side of the fence. Stop killing black people. Do the right thing and join us."

I took a deep breath and calmly said, "Ma'am, first of all, I am not ashamed of what I am doing. I am proud to be a police officer, and I am proud to be serving my community. Second, we are not killing black people, and for you to say that is irresponsible and insulting. Let me ask you this, what do you think would happen if there were no police in this city or in this country? Let me make it more personal, how would you deal with an armed intruder inside your home?"

"This world would be a better place if we didn't have cops," the woman said without a moment of pause or rational thought. "You are all racist, and all you people do is harass and kill black people. And as for the person inside my house, I would have a conversation with them and let them know that there are other options."

At that moment, a bystander spoke up. A black female in her midtwenties looked directly at the Asian lady and said in a stern voice, "Lady, you have absolutely no fucking clue about racism, and you don't know what the fuck you're talking about."

The black woman proceeded to educate the Asian woman about racism and how racism was not an issue in Portland.

Five minutes later she wrapped up her passionate monologue by saying, "Oh, and if you don't like cops, you can go live in a country where they truly have corrupt cops or no cops at all."

For the first time since the riots began, I felt my lips form a big smile. I thanked the stranger for interjecting.

"Hey, we support you guys," she said calmly. "What these people are doing, destroying businesses and rioting, is not right."

Now it's day 96 and I'm sitting in my police car in the parking garage of the TriMet contact office, a place where officers from multiple agencies are housed who deal with public transportation. I turn up my radio to hear updates on the growing crowd gathering just outside Teddy's house. I massage my aching legs and arms with my baton and wonder if this chaos will ever end. Soreness radiating throughout my body has been threatening to keep me in bed for a few days. That would be a welcome event, as the longest amount of sleep I have had since the riot started is six hours.

An officer hobbling by to use the latrine pauses and says, "Tommy, you ready for another night of craziness? I hear they are throwing rocks and bottles already."

"You look as tired and sore as I feel," I said. "I'm ready. Not that we have much of a choice, do we? My goal tonight is to try to only get one injury." For about ten minutes we compare scars and bruises from our recent encounters with rioters, who each night only get more violent and more organized.

Just as I'm about to roll up a sleeve to show him another scar, we hear our sergeant yell, "Everybody load up, they are asking for us. There's a large crowd on Twelfth and Glisan. Let's go."

I sheath my baton and place my helmet on my head. I take slow, deliberate steps toward the squad car and feel every movement as my aching muscles scream, "Sit back down, you old fool! You're gonna hurt yourself!"

I tell myself I am still young, and I have yet to reach my prime—but the aches and soreness throughout my body tell me I am as much a liar as the folks who say these violent riots are a peaceful protest.

I jump into a squad car. Within minutes we reach our staging area, which is about four blocks from the crowd. Climbing slowly out of the car, I feel pain in my right knee from catching a rock a few nights before.

A sergeant from another squad informs everyone via radio that a dental building is on fire and multiple projectiles are being thrown at his squad.

We quickly make our line from one sidewalk to the other and steadily walk toward the sound of the crowd. I can hear the blare of the sound truck giving lawful orders of dispersal and multiple force warnings to the violent crowd.

We round the corner, and the crowd is now clearly visible about two blocks away. The crowd consists of people wearing masks, gas masks, protective equipment, and helmets. Some are holding large shields. Fires are raging on both sides of the street, and the crowd continues to throw paint balloons and other projectiles toward the other squad. The crowd sees us and immediately starts throwing bottles and rocks our direction.

We stop half a block away from the crowd and wait. A frozen water bottle breaks the glare of the street lamps as it tumbles through the air straight toward my face shield. I catch the bottle with my left hand and throw it under a parked car.

I check the strap on my helmet and lower my face shield closer to my chin. The sound truck continues to give lawful orders to walk southbound, but the crowd remains defiant and refuses to leave the intersection.

A few individuals with their own megaphones yell back, "Fuck you, pigs!" and "Go home to your fat, ugly wives, no one called you here."

I recall speaking to a toddler earlier today who was more mature than that.

The crowd continues to hold the intersection as multiple subjects attempt to light another garbage can on fire. Other subjects with skateboards use their four-wheeled friends like baseball bats to shatter windows of businesses from one street corner to the other. I take mental notes of who is throwing projectiles or actively vandalizing property. Everyone is dressed in black and wearing gas masks, but shoes, patches, and other identifying marks will later betray them, and I will be there to collect.

Incident Command finally gives the order to begin making arrests.

Soreness and aches leave my body as adrenaline flows into my bloodstream. Fight or flight? Tonight, like every night prior since the riots began, it is all fight. It is all fight to protect myself and other police officers from metal-pipe-wielding, aggressive, and combative subjects who have lost complete respect for law and order.

I take off running and focus my attention on a group of individuals throwing projectiles. The crowd immediately reacts to the wave of officers barreling toward them like a Persian Army and begin to run in all directions in a state of panic.

Like a lion hunting prey, I lower my profile and ignore the rest of the fleeing miscreants as I continue to keep my eyes on a group of particularly destructive rioters. As I turn up the speed to close the final distance, I notice a large male in a white shirt running away from officers behind him—and right toward me.

Shit, I am going to collide with this behemoth! I think as I lower my shoulder and brace myself for impact.

Within a split second, we collide. The man falls flat on his back. His camera hits the ground and shatters into many pieces.

"I'm media! I'm media!" he yells before picking up the broken pieces of his camera and scurrying away toward the sidewalk.

A lot of rioters pretend to be media to avoid arrest, but right now I do not have the time to check. I quickly regain my balance and continue to sprint toward the group of males in dark clothing wrapped in protective padding from head to toe.

As I begin to close in on a white male with a skateboard running just a few steps ahead of me, I realize someone is paralleling my movements. These cowards normally run away at the first sign of conflict, but this one is running with me and toward me. He is wearing all black clothing just like the rest of his pack, gas mask on his face, and a bicycle helmet on his head. He is shadowing my every move from ten feet away to my right.

Unfortunately for him, I am fully aware of his game plan, which I have seen multiple times. Based on previous engagements with other violent rioters, I have learned a few of the tactics they have employed during the ninety-plus days of violent protests.

This guy is either blocking my path to prevent me from catching the guy with the skateboard or waiting for me to engage the guy with the skateboard so he can attack me from behind. Because of this tactic many officers—including myself—have suffered injuries from assaults during the process of making arrests.

I say under my breath, *Not this time.*

The gas-mask-wearing male locks eyes with me as we continue to run, and I faintly hear a hard breathing coming from the inside of his mask. I shift my direction, turn on the afterburners, and rapidly close the distance between us.

He stiff-arms me with his left hand and grabs my vest with the other.

This guy is actually trying to pull me down, I think to myself. I grab his clothing by the armpits and use the forward momentum I generated to push him backward. His feet go up into the air by my head, and I continue to drive forward with my momentum and pin his back to the pavement. I land on the side-mount position with my knees on the pavement. I'm sure my knees will complain later.

Immediately, the coward pushes on my chest, and I feel his knee against my side.

"Stop resisting," I order as I move to gain a more dominant position.

He throws a punch at my face. The blow on my face shield snaps my chin strap and sends my helmet flying.

Instinctively, I direct my weight on his body, and from a side-mount position I start to punch the side of his helmet.

Any moment now I am going to catch a bottle or a rock to my exposed head. I need to get him handcuffed as soon as possible.

After a few blows to gain his compliance, I transition to a knee ride (my left knee on his stomach) and repeatedly say, "Stop fighting."

"I'm not fighting you," he finally concedes as I feel his body go limp under the weight of my knee.

I attempt to remove his helmet and gas mask, and for the first time I notice another officer holding his legs. Members of my squad form a human shield around my subject as a single balloon filled with paint rockets through the air and hits my left leg. I turn the subject over and zip-tie his hands behind his back.

Another officer walks by and points a can of pepper spray to my arrestee's face and says, "Is he still resisting?"

"Not anymore," I say. "I think we are good."

The officer quickly turns around and directs his attention to the crowd that's refusing to leave. I pull my subject to his feet and pick up my helmet from the ground.

"Don't worry, man," someone yells from the crowd, "we got it on film."

Someone else shouts, "He's a medic!"

A riot medic. That's a profession I've never heard of before.

My partner and I walk Mr. John Doe around the block by the detective's van, and I begin to go through his pockets.

"Why are you arresting me, officer?" the subject asks.

"Well, for starters I'm arresting you for attempting to assault a police officer and for disorderly conduct and other charges. Now what's your name?"

"I don't have to give you my name," he says stiffly. "I know my rights and I do not need to give any officers my name."

I continue to search his pockets. "I guess you don't, but detectives will eventually identify you."

"Officer, you don't have the right to go through my pockets," he says defiantly, "and I do not give you consent to go through my pockets."

"Listen, I am not gonna argue with you about what I can and cannot do as a police officer. You are under arrest, and I have every right to search you before placing you inside the van." I finish searching Mr. John Doe's pockets and place his property in a plastic bag. I give a quick brief to the detectives and inform them of the charges. As I walk with my partner to rejoin our squad, I notice the wire to my radio pack set dangling by my leg.

"Shit, I think he ripped the wire to my radio."

"It's okay, I got a radio," my partner says. "I'll let you know if anything important comes through."

I remove the earpiece from my left ear and let it dangle over my shoulder. I guess I won't be needing it for the rest of the evening. I check my pants and notice both pant legs are ripped open at knee level. Through the holes I can see blood covering my knees and running down toward my ankles.

My first injury for the night. I'm sure there will be a few more before the shift is over.

The scattered crowd is trying to regroup. I dive into my right cargo pocket and pull out a walkie-talkie dropped by an Antifa member about a month ago. I search the channels, and after a few clicks I hear the chatter on their channel.

"Is everyone okay? We are at Eleventh and Irving, where is everyone at?"

We follow the directions given to us from the other end of the walkie-talkie and continue dispersing the crowd. We play the cat and mouse game for the next thirty minutes and make a few more arrests. Our vehicle is now covered with paint, eggs, and other unidentified liquid smeared on the windows.

One Antifa member makes a move to douse a buddy of mine, sitting in the front passenger seat of the squad car, with urine from a nozzled water bottle. He is so consumed with his evil intent that he fails to notice the officer sitting behind the front passenger seat who is armed with a large can of pepper spray.

As the subject points the nozzle of the urine-filled bottle toward our squad car, my partner showers him with pepper spray as we continue to drive. In normal circumstances we would stop and make the necessary arrest, but it's too danger-ous to stop—our squad car is being pelted by rocks and bottles.

A few minutes later Incident Command orders us to return to the contact office for a much-needed break. We arrive at the parking lot, and I remove my vest and helmet. My shirt is soaked with sweat and my vest covered in paint. I sit in the car for a few minutes with my eyes closed and feel the adrenaline leaving my body.

With my eyes closed I begin to lose consciousness when my sergeant knocks on the window.

I unroll the window.

"Hey," he says, "they posted a video of you tackling that dude, and there's already over two hundred thousand views. I'm on the phone with Incident Command about it."

"Great. I'm sure I'll get crucified for this, even though he punched me in the face."

We wait for about an hour inside the parking garage when Incident Command tells us to return to our precinct. I guess Antifa and BLM are calling it a night. I put on my vest and throw the rest of my gear in the back of the squad car. The quiet ride back to East Precinct lulls me into a deep sleep as I dream about chasing Antifa and BLM. *Stop! You're under arrest!* I yell in my dream.

I wake to my partner shaking my shoulder.

"We're home," he says. "Time to write."

I guess the guy in my dream I'm trying to arrest will get away for now.

For the next two hours or more we all sit in front of computers and write our Use of Force Reports, which will end our twelve-to fourteen-hour shifts. Most of the people we arrested will be out of jail before our shift is over. Some of us will get about two to three hours of sleep before going to court the following morning. This is a routine we have kept for the last three months.

I finish my reports and notify the sergeant they are done.

He reviews the reports and tells me we will go over it more in detail tomorrow at the beginning of the shift. I struggle up the steps and into the locker room.

I take off all my clothing and walk to the shower. I take a cold shower and wash off the dried blood around my knees and lower legs. I stand under the shower for about five more minutes with my eyes closed letting the cold water massage my sore muscles. I put on clothes as fast as my sore muscles will allow, knowing I'll be back in this locker room within a few hours.

As I fight to keep my eyes open on the drive home, I take a reassuring glance at the Sig Sauer P320 lying on the passenger seat of my truck.

Since the beginning of the riots many of us have been followed home from the precinct after our shifts. Members of Antifa and BLM have threatened to rape female officers or the wives of male officers. Others have made threats to burn down our homes or kill police officers.

I look at my rearview mirror to make sure I'm not being followed before making my next turn. I pull into my garage and walk straight to my bedroom and throw myself on my bed. Within seconds I fall into a deep asleep.

A few hours later I'm back at the precinct. I lie on the gym floor to stretch my legs when my cell phone rings. I look at the phone and see that it's the union president.

"Hey, Tommy, are you at the precinct?"

"I am."

"I'm on my way to talk to you, but the mayor is demanding you're pulled off the street. He wants your gun and badge, but we told him there's a process for that. More to follow, I'll be there before roll call."

My sergeant then pulls me into his office and confirms what the union president just informed me.

Thirty minutes later the union president arrives and tells me that I will no longer be on the street and effective immediately I am assigned to the Telephone Reporting Unit (TRU).

"Whose decision was this to pull me off the street?" I asked.

"It was the chief's office."

I shake my head in disbelief. "So I am being punished for doing what I was ordered to do and for defending myself against an aggressive person who was resisting arrest."

He nods in agreement, then says, "Just lay low for now and let's see what happens next. This will give you the opportunity to take some time off the street. I know you've been working every day since this started."

Not the answer I was looking for. And TRU is not the place to be if you're a cop who enjoys police work. Over the years TRU has served as a dumping ground for officers who have been disciplined for unfavorable actions and have been reduced to taking low-priority calls by phone.

It's a place some officers finish their careers—and a place where I never imagined I would find myself.

In a display of support, my sergeant requests that I be retained at East Precinct to take my low-priority calls, instead of physically being in TRU. The request is granted, and I find myself inside the front lobby office staring at the phone.

In my eleven years as a police officer, I've never had any problems with excessive force or had any sustained use of force complaint. Now I find myself being punished due to lack of support from a chief's office that is deeply entangled in the city's political web. I assume the chief's office folded like a wet paper bag under the pressure from politically driven members of the city council and the mayor's office.

I sit by the phone for an hour before going back to the sergeant's office and requesting to have the rest of the day off.

"Done." The sergeant smiles weakly and says, "I don't blame you. Take the rest of the day off and get some rest. Don't worry about the riots tonight, we got it."

As I walk back to the locker room, the words *The chief wants your gun and badge* run repeatedly through my head.

The Democratic Ted Wheeler, the district attorney, and city council have repeatedly attacked the character of every member of the Portland Police Bureau. They have accused us of being racist and heavy-handed. Worst of all, city council member Jo Ann Hardesty accused us of setting fires in Portland during the riots.

They sit in positions that are way beyond their qualifications or capabilities. Their poor decision-making lacks the benefit of intellect, vision, and critical thinking, and their inability to lead has driven the city into our current unrecognizable state. How they continue to stay in power is a question I can't answer.

I have seen bad leaders in the military, and I continue to see bad leaders in the military, but they cannot begin to compete with the level of incompetence shown by the leadership of the city of Portland.

I can only hope and pray that the citizens of this city will begin to see that the people they voted into office do not have their best interests at heart.

Wake up, Portland, before it is too late.

CHAPTER 10

THE LONG WAIT

June 15, 2021

It is eleven months after my reassignment to TRU, and I am in Germany serving as an Operations Officer/Battle Major inside the Mission Command Center's Current Operations Intelligence Center (COIC) for U.S. Army Europe-Africa (USAREUR-AF). I took the position six months ago.

Before leaving the United States, I was informed that the Portland district attorney's office was investigating my use of force on Tyler Cox, the person I took to the ground the night of Mayor Wheeler's fifty-eighth birthday, August 31, 2020.

Nearly a year after the incident, the DA still has not made a decision on my case.

If I had not taken this position in Germany, I would still be sitting inside the Telephone Reporting Unit taking cold calls for ten hours a day.

My phone rings, and it's a friend of mine from the Riot Response Team.

"Hey, man," he says, "I'm sure you've heard about Corey. Rotten deal."

He's right, I have heard. In fact, I've been trolling the media for weeks looking for news on Corey's indictment.

I know Officer Corey Budworth personally. Good man and good cop with the Portland Police Bureau.

A few days ago, a grand jury declared him guilty of fourth degree assault.

Fourth degree assault is defined by the Oregon Revised Statute (ORS) 163.160 as occurring when a person intentionally, knowingly, or recklessly causes physical injury to another, or when criminal negligence causes physical injury to another by means of a deadly weapon.[7]

The incident in question took place August 18, 2020, when we responded to a riot at the Multnomah Building near downtown Portland. After subjects were seen breaking windows and a Molotov cocktail was thrown inside the Multnomah Building, officers—including Officer Budworth, myself, and others—were ordered by Incident Command to clear the area.

Here's how we do that: Multiple warnings are given to disperse, but what often takes place (and what took place all summer in Portland) is that protesters defy that order. When that happens, we line the street from one sidewalk to another and push the crowd in a direction preselected by Incident Command.

And that's exactly what was going down on August 18, 2020.

While we were conducting "the push," rioters displayed an absolute disregard for law and order by pushing back, punching, throwing projectiles, and pepper spraying officers.

While Officer Budworth was attempting to move one woman, she stumbled and fell to the ground. As she attempted to get up, she came up beneath Budworth's baton and caught a push to the back of her head.[8]

And this is what the jury deemed intentionally, knowingly, or recklessly causing physical injury to another.

"Yeah, I heard about Corey," I tell my friend on the phone, "and it is very disappointing. I've heard that other agencies are no longer offering their services for fear of being prosecuted by the DA if they have to take action against rioters."

My friend says this is true.

"If you want my honest opinion," I add, "you all need to quit the team to show your support to Corey—and before the rest of you end up indicted. There's already a few of us who are under investigation, let's not add more. This team is a voluntary position, there's no requirement for anyone to stay especially when you have a DA who is seeking to indict officers."

My friend takes a deep breath and after a moment says, "Yeah, I totally agree with you. We have a team meeting tonight, and after talking with a few members, I believe that's where we are headed. I think we are going to disband the team. There's a few who don't agree, but the vast majority wants to quit. I'll keep you posted."

For a brief moment, anger flares inside me as I think about the DA's aggressive campaign to prosecute police officers for their actions in the ongoing battle with Antifa and BLM. Instead of prosecuting those breaking the law, he has diverted his efforts to scrutinizing any and all use of police force—even incidents that have already been investigated and cleared by the Portland Police Bureau.

"This shouldn't be a meeting to decide if the team should quit," I say, taking a breath to help my anger dissipate. "This should be a meeting to decide how soon you all can turn in your gear. The conditions this city demands we work under are already unsafe, and now we are risking prosecution every time we respond to the nightly riots. This is the time to band together and fight back. Disband the team and let the city figure out a solution to the problem they have created."

That night, I go to sleep thinking of all the hours I have spent in the daily defense of Portland from Antifa and BLM. I think about the fact there are simply unavoidable uses of force when officers are given the job of apprehending violent protesters with ill intent toward police officers and others. We have little choice when defending ourselves and the public against violent threats of serious physical injury or death.

These uses of force are not taken lightly for many reasons. Indeed, the administrative process, report writing, and mandatory interviews with supervisors that surround a single use-of-force event are enough in themselves to discourage officers from using force at all during an arrest.

My thoughts slowly fade as I give into exhaustion.

Six hours later, my eardrums are assaulted by the alarm on my cell phone. I jerk awake. Wiping the drool from my mouth, I grab my phone and disable the alarm. I check my messages, and one in particular from a friend and coworker catches my eye: DONE. WE ALL RESIGNED FROM THE TEAM.

Local and mainstream media corroborate the news. Headlines announce that approximately fifty members of the Riot Response Team voted to disband the team.

I pick up my phone to call another friend who is part of the team.

"Hey, brother," I greet him after he picks up. "So how was the team meeting? I'm reading the articles now."

"It went well," he says. "We voted and that was all to it. Everyone pretty much stated the same reasons for quitting, and that's because of the lack of support from the mayor and the district attorney. We all have worked very hard to protect the city, and we deserve better. We could have done this for the next year or longer if we could have had the support from our city leaders. With the new DA looking for reasons to put a cop in the slammer, we have to draw the line somewhere. How about you, man, have you heard anything about your case?"

"No, but I have a feeling something is about to come out with all the stuff that's going on and with Corey's ruling. I'm so glad I didn't stick around—sitting in TRU for ten months would have killed my passion for police work. I know some cops don't mind finishing their careers in an office, but I'm not built for that."

"I still can't figure out why you were pushed to TRU when other officers in the same boat get to stay on their beats."

"Me neither—unless it's because the video of me taking down Tyler Cox went viral. In any case, I'm glad you guys made the decision to disband the team, and I am sure most officers in the Bureau support that decision. The way things are right now, we are going to continue to deal with lawsuits for the year to come. Every use of force will translate to another lawsuit. That's just how it is in this city. People know the city will settle most lawsuits, and it's an easy pot of money for people to stick their hands in."

We continue to talk about the riots for another minute before addressing the issue of gun violence. I wasn't surprised at all by my friend's description of the current state of affairs.

"Shootings are out of control," he said. "We can't keep up with it. With our Gun Violence Reduction Team gone, gangsters are running the streets unchallenged. Believe it or not, the city is trying to develop a new team to combat gun violence."

Just last summer the city voted to defund the Gun Violence Reduction Team (GVRT). The result of that poor decision by incompetent city politicians has been—surprise, surprise!—an exponential rise in gun violence, much of which victimizes young black teenagers involved in gangs and perpetrated by rival gangs.

Now the city wants to fund a new team to combat gun violence?

"You're joking, right?" I shake my head.

"I wish. It's called Focused Intervention Team (FIT), and it will have civilian oversight. Can you imagine having civilians with no law enforcement background making decisions on what they think you can and cannot do? No thank you. I don't think anyone is interested in joining the team."

We wrap up our conversation and get off the phone. As I get dressed for work, I wonder if the thought ever crosses the minds of our politicians that maybe they should not have dissolved the Gun Violence Reduction Team. Logic would say that if you remove an asset that is specifically design to reduce or prevent the occurrence of crime, the natural consequence will be a rise in the thing that asset was designed to prevent. Unfortunately, logic and critical thinking do not influence the thoughts and actions of Portland's current administration, especially Jo Ann Hardesty, the person who pushed the hardest to dismantle our GVRT.

I consider it a tragedy that the mayor, city council, and district attorney not only will never be held accountable for their actions but will continue to make decisions that hurt the community and put lives at risk.

I can say with the utmost confidence that some of the lives lost due to the escalation in gun violence are attributed to the mayor and city council's decision to disband the Gun Violence Reduction Team.

June 25, 2021

Ten days after my friend Corey received an indictment for assault in the fourth degree, I wake up to multiple text messages with links to a news story that hits even closer to home.

According to the *Willamette Week*, "The Multnomah County District Attorney's office is considering criminal prosecution for Portland Police Bureau Officer Thomas Clark, believed to be the officer who tackled and punched volunteer medic Tyler Cox during an August 2020 protest."[9]

The article also mentions that Tyler Cox is an ICU nurse at the Oregon Health and Science University (OHSU) hospital in Portland.

In other words, Tyler Cox, a volunteer "protest medic," is an ICU nurse who repeatedly placed himself among thousands of people during the height of COVID while remaining in contact with vulnerable patients in the Intensive Care Unit at OHSU. The fact that he is still employed by OHSU after participating in a riot is a failure of the hospital's administration. Considering the environment that he placed himself in and his current profession, one can only hope that he was not an asymptomatic COVID-19 carrier and that he did not infect any of the patients with whom he came in contact at the hospital.

The news of a possible prosecution by the DA does not surprise me. It's something I had suspected a few months after the incident, especially when the union assigned me a defense attorney—a superb criminal defense specialist I worked with in 2015 when I was forced to shoot a knife-wielding male in self-defense.

I forward the link to my attorney and add in the text message, HAVE YOU SEEN THIS? I GUESS THERE'S NO MORE GUESSING.

Throughout the morning I continue to receive messages from friends and coworkers regarding the article. I'm sure my mother will be calling me soon.

A few minutes later my phone rings.

"Hey, son, are you going to jail?"

"No, Mom, I'm not going to jail. The article simply states that the DA is considering prosecution, nothing more.

If he decides to prosecute, I will go before a grand jury, just like my friend Corey. If the grand jury finds me guilty, then I will have to go to trial. That is pretty much how it works."

"Oh, okay," she says. "That's good, still a chance then."

My poor mother. There was a point in my career when I told her I was a "mall cop" so she wouldn't worry about me so much. She figured out I was lying when she saw me on the news holding a rifle on the side of the road. It was hard to come up with a cover story at that point. I also did not think she actually believed me when I told her I was a mall cop, but seeing the surprised look on her face when she saw me on the news with a rifle made me feel terrible about misleading my own mother. I eventually had to explain to her that I was on a perimeter and that we were looking for a shooter who had shot someone with a pistol.

Three months later I told her I was a parking patrol officer, and she said, "Yeah, whatever, you can't fool me twice."

After reading the article, I ponder the chain of events that took place August 31, 2020, the events that led to my confrontation of Tyler Cox. I view the event from the eyes of the district attorney, a prosecutor seeking to find criminal misconduct on my part during the arrest of Tyler Cox.

I rewatch the video posted by Andy Ngo on Twitter, in which it is clearly evident that Tyler Cox resisted arrest, struck me on the face, and knocked off my helmet. Punching Cox on the side of his helmet after receiving a punch to my face was an attempt to gain compliance in a rapidly evolving situation.[10] It was a tactic that was absolutely necessary to control a combative subject like Tyler Cox.

For those who have never experienced violence or have never had to defend themselves personally or someone else against violent aggression, it might be difficult to understand the actions I took against Mr. Cox.

People who oppose all violence fail to understand or forget that police officers are hired to do exactly that—to be "violent" on their behalf so they don't have to.

Police officers are often placed in situations where "violence" is necessary for the survival of others or themselves. Officers who are incapable of "violence" endanger not only themselves but other officers and the public they are sworn to protect. Officers are trained to use the least amount of force to effect arrest. But to an untrained person, any level of force may appear to be excessive.

Seeing me punch Mr. Cox on his helmet, no matter how hard, may translate as a grossly violent event to people who do not believe in violence, not even as self-defense. They can interpret any level of force as "excessive force," a term the media seems to have made synonymous with "police officer."[11]

Seeing violence in real life is much different than watching the choreographed fight scenes featuring Jean-Claude Van Damme or John Wick. Force, or "violence," has real consequences, and unfortunately it is sometimes necessary for the survival of officers when faced with violent criminals or hate-filled rioters with malicious intent.

The fact that the DA could insinuate that I may have acted beyond the scope of my duties is an insult and a huge disservice to every officer who has worked night after night

THE 2020 PORTLAND RIOTS

to defend the city of Portland—or any city, for that matter—against Antifa and BLM.

Since day one of the riots, we have been exposed to slander, verbal harassment, fireworks, Molotov cocktails, projectiles, pepper spray, balloons filled with urine and feces, threats of serious physical injury or death, threats of sexual assaults, racism, and much more. Many officers have suffered serious physical injuries, and some will not return to duty.

Despite the many atrocities we faced from Antifa and BLM, however, we returned night after night to protect the businesses and citizens of Portland.

It's a fact that the DA and the mayor have completely ignored.

Chapter 11

THE CIVIL LAWSUIT

July 1, 2021

Six days after Mike Schmidt's announcement of a possible prosecution in regard to my actions against Cox, a friend of mine sends me a link to a new article.

This one states that Tyler Cox has filed a lawsuit against the city claiming that I violated his constitutional rights on August 31, 2020. The lawsuit alleges that I slammed Cox's head on the pavement and punched him with "raised plastic knuckles intended to inflict more damage to victim." The lawsuit also alleges that I fabricated the arrest and used excessive force on Cox. Cox is claiming he suffered permanent and debilitating injuries to include traumatic brain injury, bruising on his forehead near his scalp, sprains to his shoulder and neck, and aggravation to a preexisting lower back injury. Furthermore, Cox stated that he suffers from anxiety and PTSD and has sought mental health treatment. Cox also stated that he suffered wage loss due to his brain injury, which forced him to take seven weeks of "brain rest."

I read the article several times while shaking my head in disbelief and disgust. The entire lawsuit is a lie. It is embarrassingly obvious that Cox's attorney did not do his homework, even though he had access to the most convincing evidence of all, the video.

Play the video in slow motion or frame by frame and it is clear that Cox's head did not hit the pavement.

Cox immediately tucked his chin to his chest prior to impact, a reaction that he may have instinctively or accidently employed, preventing the back of his helmet from striking the pavement. The punches I delivered to his helmet to attempt to gain his compliance were definitely not hard enough to inflict injuries that would warrant "brain rest."

Even if his head was fully exposed and without the protection of his bicycle helmet, his cranium would have protected his brain from the low level of energy I placed behind the punches. Punches thrown were delivered to get his attention and provide a warning that further resistance would elicit an escalated level of controlled violence—not to inflict physical pain or disfigurement. The tactic worked, and it prevented Cox from escalating into a level of aggression that would not have benefited him in any way possible. For him to claim traumatic brain injury is a disservice to those who have legitimately suffered TBI.

On September 2, 2020, two days after the incident where Cox falsely claims that I was wearing gloves with raised plastic knuckles, a video surfaced of him conducting an interview with a reporter from KATU news. It's not surprising that the media portrayed him as a victim and not once asked the more relevant question, "What was a nurse doing in the middle of a riot dressed in protective equipment and disobeying lawful order to disperse?" The average person does not go out to peacefully protest by wearing pads and a helmet. It was evident from day one that some of the George Floyd demonstrations across the United States were synonymous with violence and hatred toward law enforcement. Cox playing the victim's card and crying in front of a camera does not excuse his participation and actions during the riots and—more importantly—does not warrant a pass from the DA's office.

All charges against Cox were dropped by the DA's office. Once again, the DA sent a clear message that rioting and willful disregard of law and order is permissible in the city of Portland. Cox was given a lawful order to leave an area where criminal activities were taking place, and he made the conscious decision to remain and disobey that lawful order.

When the lawsuit came out, Cox's attorney provided a picture of me wearing olive-and-gray gloves with padded knuckles. He did it to support the claim that the gloves are intended to cause pain to suspects and that I was wearing those gloves when confronting Cox.

There are two things that are misleading about that photo:

1. Wearing gloves with padded plastic knuckles is the same as wearing elbow pads, knee pads, helmets, and other protective equipment. Plastic knuckles in gloves protect the delicate bones of the hand from scrapes

and blunt trauma from projectiles like rocks and bottles, just two of the many objects thrown at police officers during the riots. They are used for protecting vulnerable areas of the body, not as an offensive tool to inflict damage. To suggest that officers wear gloves with raised knuckles to inflict pain or damage is foolish, inflammatory, and should not tolerated. In fact, the accusation shows an astonishing lack of knowledge.

2. The photo of me wearing the olive-and-gray padded gloves with plastic knuckles was taken during a riot a few months *prior* to the incident with Tyler Cox.

During the riots, for a time I wore the gloves with protective plastic over the knuckles due to an injury I received from a violent rioter. I had a wound over one of my fingers close to the knuckle that would reopen every time we had to put our hands on someone to make an arrest. When the wound finally healed, I replaced the padded gloves with a pair of thin black cotton gloves that made it possible for me to search a subject without taking off my gloves.

I was wearing the thin black gloves when I made contact with Cox the night of Mayor Wheeler's birthday.

Cox's attorney completely missed or willfully disregarded all of the above facts in an effort to paint a picture of police brutality.

There are others like Cox who were arrested during the riots and have filed lawsuits against the city. The details of each lawsuit may be different, but what each case has in common is the defendant's decision to participate in pro-tests that not only turned violent but led to the destruction of multiple businesses and other properties in the city of Portland. Many of these people will never take ownership for their own actions, yet they expect compensation because they left police with no other choice but to use force to overcome their resistance, aggression, and blatant disregard for law and order.

Unfortunately, a lot of these lawsuits will be settled out of court because settling will cost the city less money than the cost of going to trial. In fact, it is not uncommon for a person to file lawsuits against the city two or more times knowing the city will pay for them to go away.

Police officers have very little input in the decision to settle or take the civil lawsuit to trial. This decision is based not on principle but cost-benefit analysis. Money managers are extremely risk adverse, which provides opportunities for people like Cox to tap into taxpayers' pockets. The result is that money that city leaders could use to better the community are, in many cases, used instead to reward poor decision making and criminal behavior.

For example, May 10, 2017, Officer Samson Ajir shot and killed Terrel Johnson in what a grand jury found as "a lawful exercise of self-defense" under criminal law.[12] A few years later, July 2021, Portland City Council unanimously approved a $600,000 settlement agreement to the family of Terrel Johnson.[13] Officer Ajir acted in a manner to protect himself from serious physical injury or death from a man who was armed with an edged weapon. Despite being cleared from any criminal wrong doing, and having acted in self defense, Officer Ajir's actions were overshadowed by the city's decision to reward Terrel Jonhnson's family.

There's a good percentage of officers who will be involved in multiple civil lawsuits if they stick around long enough to see retirement. Some officers experience their first lawsuit shortly in the first six months of duty. It is the nature of our profession, and that is why it is incumbent upon officers to conduct themselves professionally and execute the power given to them within the parameters of the law.

Yet, despite following the law and executing their duties with the highest level of professionalism, officers are still vulnerable to civil lawsuits, criminal allegations, and complaints. There are simply those who hold animosity toward law enforcement and will latch on to the first opportunity to file a complaint or a lawsuit.

This is not my first civil lawsuit and most definitely will not be my last.

There have been many instances I wished I had a body camera, which would have prevented false claims and frivolous lawsuits from ever reaching the courthouse. In fact, the Portland Police Bureau has made numerous attempts to secure body cameras for police officers, but the city of Portland continues to present excuses—including not having enough money—to keep that from happening. It is my opinion that the city does not want to fund body cams for officers because the incendiary and divisive rhetoric of politicians and the media would crumble under the lens of truth, proving them to be nothing but liars and agitators.

The media and politicians play a significant role when it comes to civil lawsuits and criminal proceedings against police officers. The constant demonizing of police officers by media and politicians continues to fuel the flames of hate, and often a guilty verdict is given by the media and politicians before trial even begins.

There are those who are easily influenced by the rhetoric of the media. Due to the constant spoon-feeding from the media, a vulnerable portion of our population foolishly believe that every encounter with law enforcement is fodder for a legitimate lawsuit or complaint. Independent thinkers are rarer today than an honest politician and are often labeled as either racist or an extremist for demonstrating the ability to ask questions. The mainstream media is like a one-way street: information flows in one direction and wrong-way drivers are not tolerated. Unfortunately, most media consumers are simply going with the flow and never question the validity of what they hear and see.

As for Mr. Cox, I am confident that he feels vindicated due to the way he was coddled by the media. The way he portrayed himself during his interview was in stark contrast to how he behaved toward law enforcement the night he was arrested for failing to obey lawful orders. On the night of our confrontation, Cox was extremely uncooperative and antagonistic toward officers and detectives. He remained defiant in his belief that officers had no legal right to arrest him.

In addition, the Cox that I spoke to after the incident was not suffering from traumatic brain injury or any debilitating injuries. I have personally seen the effects of traumatic brain injury, and Mr. Cox did not exhibit any of those symptoms. Mr. Cox was completely aware of the situation he was in and immediately turned into a street lawyer and attempted to lecture me on "illegal search" and "illegal arrest."

The soft spoken, fake-crying Mr. Cox we saw after the fact on television was not present on the night I arrested him, but I suspect that's the Mr. Cox we'll see during the trial.

If there's a trial.

And I sincerely hope there is.

To settle out of court with Mr. Cox would only solidify the notion that the city of Portland not only tolerates lawlessness but also empowers people to victimize the city's financial resources.

Law-abiding, taxpaying citizens of our great country deserve better than that.

Chapter 12

CRIMINAL INVESTIGATION ANALYSIS

September 1, 2021

It's been one year since I was removed from the streets for doing what I was commanded to do by Incident Command. And I'm not alone. Many officers have been or are being investigated for their actions during the riots, actions directed by Incident Command based on their assessment of information given to them by leaders on the ground.

The fact that these actions were ordered by Incident Command is crucial.

Independent action by officers is completely prohibited unless an event requires an officer to intervene to prevent serious physical injury or death. Every night before we traveled in convoy to face violence perpetrated by Antifa and BLM, we reminded each other to take all commands from the tower, take no independent action, and to protect each other. These are rules we followed meticulously, especially considering the political atmosphere and volatile situations to which we were exposed daily.

Considering the many investigations into the actions of Portland police officers who sacrificed their safety to prevent the city of Portland from total destruction, there is a glaring void: not one person from Incident Command has been investigated for their role and decisions during the riots.

To focus the blame solely on the officers on the ground is a concept that is completely foreign to me. I say this based on spending more than two decades in the military and serving in many leadership roles. In the military, leaders are held accountable for actions taken at the lowest level under their command. Commanders have been relieved of duty for poor decision-making by their subordinate leaders. This is the one of the reasons why we are the greatest military in the world: we hold leaders accountable and, more importantly, we hold each other accountable.

Officers on the ground executed commands given by Incident Command and defended themselves when needed. The level of violence we faced on a nightly basis has been one of the worst this country has ever seen. The duration of the 2020 Portland riots was the longest in the history of the United States, and we may never see the likes of it again in our lifetime.

For personal and career reasons, no officer wants to engage in nightly physical confrontation, risking serious injury or even death. One injury can end an officer's career or permanently remove him or her from the streets. The idea that officers "enjoy fighting" with protesters is completely false and an irresponsible thing to say. This level of ignorance competes with the comment by city council member Jo Ann Hardesty that officers were responsible for setting fires to the city.

A lot has happened in the world of policing since I left the city of Portland to do something more meaningful than sit in an office and make phone calls, which I consider an unjust punishment for taking actions against lawbreakers as directed by Incident Command.

Looking back at the things I have accomplished and learned while working as an Operations Officer / Battle Major at a four-star command, it was without a doubt a wise decision to remove from myself temporarily from the environment I was in.

The Portland Police Bureau and other departments across the United States have seen unprecedented numbers of officers leave or retire. The mass exodus is nothing less than a reflection of poor leadership and lack of support from city and department leaders at the highest level.

It also puts us all at risk. To lose good officers not only impacts the organization, but citizens of Portland and other cities will suffer due to the rise of crime and the fear of crime. In the last year, crime has risen to a level that is beyond alarming as liberal politicians continue to defund the police. Some cities like Minneapolis have requested to "refund" their police department due to the increase in violent crimes and slower response from a dwindling staff of officers.

Allowing police departments to fall below minimum staffing is a dereliction of duty, and city leaders should be held accountable. If you take away two to three players in an eleven-person soccer team, their chance of winning almost drops to zero. Another way of looking at it is this: if you remove components designed to combat crime, crime will flourish. Inexplicably, this simple concept eludes many politicians as they continue to destroy the basic foundations of law and order. And attacking police departments financially isn't all that is happening—many anti-police lawmakers are hard at work attacking the sanctity of our justice system.

In April of 2021, at the height of Derek Chauvin's trial, millions of people around the world waited on pins and needles for the verdict. While speaking at a demonstration at the Brooklyn Center in Minnesota, Congresswoman Maxine Watters announced that she wanted nothing less than a murder conviction against former officer Derek Chauvin. When she was asked what would happen if Chauvin was not convicted, Waters said, "We have gotta stay on the street, we've got to get more active, we've got to get more confrontational, we've got to make sure that they know that we mean business."

What an irresponsible thing to say prior to a pending decision by the grand jury of Derek Chauvin's trial! While it's impossible to prove that her comments influenced the outcome of the Chauvin trial, a politician should never comment on any trial and disrespect the process of the judicial government. Maxine Watters not only attacked the sanctity of the justice system, she incited violence by telling people to get more confrontational and to stay on the streets. I have seen the "confrontational" tactics of BLM and Antifa on the streets firsthand, and it can only be described as one thing: violence.

It's unlikely that Watters will ever be held accountable for her comments—but one thing we can count on is that officers will continue to be demonized by her and her constituents.

September 2021

It's about midnight and I am getting ready for bed when my phone beeps with an incoming text message.

It's a text from Steve, my attorney.

GOT THE RESULTS OF THE INVESTIGATION, WE WON. DA DECLINED TO PROSECUTE. I'LL SEND YOU THE MEMO IN YOUR EMAIL.

I stare at the text message for a few minutes before realizing I'm holding my breath. I take a few deep breaths and feel the cloud that's been looming over me for the last year dissipate.

It has taken the DA's office one year to make their decision, and for that year I would have served my punishment behind a desk if I would have chosen to stay. The DA's decision only validates what I knew all along, that I acted within the parameters of the law and the punishment given was given as a reactionary response to the video of the incident that went viral and eventually exceeded two million views.

The chief's office may argue that, when an officer is under investigation, they are protecting that officer by hiding them away behind a desk—but in my opinion the chief's office is also surrendering to political pressure by not supporting and fighting for officers who continuously put themselves at risk to protect the city.

There are few things in an organization that will force a rapid deterioration of morale and productivity more than a politically correct leader. Being politically correct does not solve problems and more importantly does not place the needs of officers in the forefront. I believe that good leaders should protect their people from the reaches of those who would use them as political pawns to drive an agenda.

After all, the most basic requirement of a good leader is to take care of his or her subordinates even if it means losing his or her job. If you lose your job because you did what was morally and legally right in order to protect your people, then you have done your job as a leader, and people will continue to serve good leaders. We have a few excellent leaders in the Bureau, and my hope is that they continue to rise as leaders and bring a change to an organization that is wallowing in leadership mediocrity.

After receiving Steve's text, I check my email and find that he has sent me the memorandum from Deputy DA Nicole Hermann to DA Mike Schmidt. I'll read it in the morning. In the meantime, I send a quick message to my night-owl mom saying, I'M GOOD, MOM. DA'S DECIDED NOT TO PROSECUTE.

I say a quick prayer and lay my head on the pillow. I feel a sense of calmness that I have not felt in a long time, and before I can check my phone for my mom's response, I am asleep.

At six a.m., I wake up to multiple text message from friends and coworkers letting me know of the media's coverage on the DA's decision regarding my case. I grab my laptop and place it on the table as I make a pot of coffee. It is time to review the document Steve sent me last night, which has now been released to the public.

The memorandum was written to DA Mike Schmidt by a deputy district attorney addressing the findings.

Opening the document, I read the first sentence, "The following memorandum is a criminal legal analysis of the actions of Portland Police Officer Thomas Clark in regards to his use of force during the arrest of Tyler Cox on August 31, 2020."

The document states the reason for the analysis: to determine whether my actions on the night I engaged Mr. Cox were lawful under Oregon criminal law.

The first paragraph addresses the deputy DA's declination to issue criminal charges, then concludes that I used justified force to control Mr. Cox.

The following paragraphs cover the topics of "probable cause," and the authority given to peace officers to use physical force when objectively reasonable.

Probable cause can be traced to the fourth amendment; it says that certain requirement must be met before a peace officer can make an arrest or conduct a search. In this case I had probable cause to arrest Tyler Cox because I had reasons to believe he committed a crime. A riot was declared during a protest, and Mr. Cox refused to leave after multiple legal orders were given to disperse. At this point Mr. Cox and others remained unlawfully assembled, and individuals within the crowd continued to engage in criminal activities by burning city property and throwing projectiles at police. The sound truck took further steps and warned the crowd that those who chose to remain would be subject to arrest and use of force by police.

The document also references House Bill 4301, Section 7, which states that "a peace officer may use physical force upon another person only when it is objectively reasonable to make a lawful arrest when there is probable cause to believe the person has committed a crime or when the officer believes a person poses an imminent threat of physical injury to the peace officer." Oregon Revised Statute (ORS) 161.209 also talks about using physical force in self-defense. These two passages are important to note as I attempt to explain the analysis made by Deputy DA Nicole Hermann.

Hermann introduces Mr. Cox as I described in my report and as seen on the video, running a few feet from me and paralleling my movement. The force I used during my encounter with Mr. Cox are broken down to three separate force events: the first force event takes place when I take Mr. Cox to the ground, the second takes place when I deliver several punches to the side of his helmet, and the third force event is when I attempt to remove his gas mask, although the report states that I attempted to remove his helmet.

In terms of the first force event, the analysis of this case focuses on whether or not my belief that Mr. Cox posed a threat was objectively reasonable and not if Mr. Cox intended to assault or injure me.

The investigation sheds light on the fact that Mr. Cox grabbed the top of my vest as soon as my hands made contact with his shoulders. This was both a sign that he was not going to comply with the arrest and a prelude to his active aggression during the arrest. Mr. Cox alleges that I intention-ally picked him up and slammed his body onto the curb. The deputy DA's report states that the video does not support Mr. Cox's allegation and that no evidence can be found to prove that I "acted intentionally to harm Mr. Cox, or that Mr. Cox was intentionally thrown down onto a curb."

For that matter, the video clearly shows Mr. Cox lying on the street and not the curb. Let me take a moment to cover the significance of the curb and why Mr. Cox is alleg-ing I slammed his head on the curb. A curb is the edge of a sidewalk next to the street. Most curbs have sharp edges to prevent vehicles from leaving the roadway where pedestrian safety is paramount. That same curb can inflict significant damages to a person's body due to its sharp edge, and the slight raise in elevation acts as a fulcrum, which can cause bones to break if enough force is exerted. I have to assume that Mr. Cox has seen the video, but maybe his mind has processed the data the way he wants to remember it. For this force event the investigation concludes that my use of force on Mr. Cox was reasonable.

The second force event is where I was seen punching Mr. Cox on the side of his helmet. Mr. Cox alleges that I repeat-edly punched him on the face with plastic reinforced knuckles on my gloves. Mr. Cox also alleges that my helmet was not properly secured during the incident and that he used very little force to catapult my helmet off my head. I highly doubt Mr. Cox was in a state of Zen where he would have had the opportunity or the wherewithal to check on the tightness of my chin strap. Furthermore, this force event took place on the ninety-sixth consecutive day of the riots, and proper wear of the helmet was part of the conditions checklist we went through prior to making contact with rioters. To counter Mr. Cox's allegation that my helmet was not properly secured during the incident, Deputy DA Hermann points out that I was seen running, I took Mr. Cox to the ground, and while attempting to control Mr. Cox, my head was bent toward the ground: "Through all of this significant movement, Officer Clark's helmet remains secured firmly in place. The helmet does not move until Mr. Cox's hands knock it off."

Now to address the most significant part of the second force event where Mr. Cox alleges he was punched in the face at least five times with raised plastic knuckles on my gloves.

Once again, I have to wonder, did Mr. Cox or his lawyer watch the video before submitting the civil lawsuit? As stated in the deputy DA's analysis, the video clearly shows I was not wearing gloves with plastic reinforced knuckles. The deputy DA's analysis states, "Medical records and photographs of Mr. Cox following the incident show that he suffered a single hematoma to the left side of his head in an area covered by both his hairline and his helmet. Small visible abrasions to Mr. Cox's forehead and hairline, near where his helmet padding would likely have been, are present in the photographs he provided. However, these small abrasions are not consistent with his description of being struck in the face five times by a person wearing gloves with plastic reinforced knuckles. The evidence is consistent with Officer Clark's statement, that Officer Clark hit Mr. Cox in the helmet, not the face."

Going back to the punches I delivered on the side of Mr. Cox's helmet, I believe it's appropriate to mention again House Bill 4301, Section 7. Considering the situation I was in, an environment that had been declared a riot, I had reasons to believe that Mr. Cox posed an imminent threat of significant injury due to his actions during the arrest. The force that I felt on my face shield led me to believe I had been punched in the face. The force was significant enough to unsnap my chin strap and catapult my helmet away from my head. This is the exact moment when I assessed that Mr. Cox could follow up with another strike to my unprotected head and face. To address the question of whether my belief that Mr. Cox posed a threat was objectively reasonable is clearly answered by the Deputy DA's analysis: "Given the environment, and Mr. Cox's behavior, Officer Clark's belief that unlawful force was being used against him was objectively reasonable."

The last use of force in the investigation focuses on the part where I attempted to remove Mr. Cox's gas mask. Mr. Cox alleges that I made numerous attempts to remove his helmet, or gas mask, indicating he sustained injuries from that attempted removal. Deputy DA Hermann's memo to DA Mike Schmidt refers to the video where I was seen pulling on Mr. Cox's mask (i.e., helmet) one time. Her memo states, "Once it was clear the helmet was not coming off, Officer Clark left it alone."

It appears that Mr. Cox has a different memory of the incident, and I am grateful the incident was captured on video. The video only reveals a part of the story, but it's definitely a necessary piece of information that can prove or disprove allegations made by either party. In this case, I alleged that Mr. Cox resisted arrest and I had reasons to believe he posed imminent threat of injury. Mr. Cox alleges I threw him onto the curb, I punched him at least five times while wearing gloves with plastic reinforced knuckles, and I made multiple attempts to remove his helmet, or gas mask. Unfortunately for Cox, video surveillance, photographs, and medical records proved his allegations to be untrue.

Deputy DA Hermann's criminal legal analysis finishes with a final statement saying, "For these reasons, Officer Clark's use of force during the arrest of Tyler Cox was justified under Oregon Law. As a result, criminal charges are not warranted in this case."

Hermann's analysis is well written and accurately depicts the event that took place involving me and Mr. Cox the night of Mayor Wheeler's birthday. I am sure a lot of hours went into this investigation, and it is unfortunate that it had to happen. I am not bitter and do not hold any animosity toward anyone, including Mr. Cox.

I understand that I am in a profession where our actions as officers will forever be under a microscope and scrutinized. What I don't understand is the blatant disrespect that I have seen toward officers in the last five years or more. There has been a large shift in the way people see law enforcement personnel, and that can be attributed to the rhetoric spewed by politicians at the highest level, the mainstream media, professional athletes, and actors—the same people who rely on personal security provided by law enforcement personnel.

If politicians and mainstream media continue to villainize good police officers, the exodus of police officers that this country is seeing now will only get worse. Crime will continue to rise at a level that will be unprecedented and law-abiding citizens across the United States will suffer the consequences.

The cancer that is crippling our great nation lies in the offices across the United States of those who hold power. Incompetent personnel with no track record to speak of are placed or voted into leadership roles or positions of power. Their inability to lead infects local government like a virus, bringing with it radical ideologies and initiatives that stifle progress and turn once-safe communities into playgrounds for criminals.

The harmful rhetoric toward police officers must stop, and that message must be delivered by leaders at the lowest and highest levels of government. Hold politicians who voted to defund the police accountable by voting them out of office before they cause further damage to the community.

People of Portland and citizens across the United States, you have the power to enforce change.

Vote wisely, and unlike Antifa and BLM, protest peacefully for change. Do this not only for yourselves but for future generations.

APPENDIX

Memorandum from Deputy DA Nicole Hermann to DA Mike Schmidt Regarding PPB Office Thomas Clark[14]

Mike Schmidt, District Attorney

1200 SW First Avenue, Suite 5200
Portland, OR 97204-1193
Phone: 503-988-3162 Fax: 503-988-3643
www.mcda.us

MEMORANDUM

To: DA Mike Schmidt
From: Nicole Hermann
Date: July 9, 2021
Subject: Review of Protest Case – PPB Officer Thomas Clark

The following memorandum is a criminal legal analysis of the actions of Portland Police Officer Thomas Clark in regards to his use of force during the arrest of Tyler Cox on August 31, 2020. The video capturing this incident was widely shared and understandably has ignited community concern in the level of force used against Mr. Cox. The MCDA acknowledges the disturbing nature of the video and the impact these images have on our community. However, it is beyond the scope of this analysis to review or address other mechanisms in place for accountability. The narrow focus of this analysis is whether Officer Clark's actions were lawful under Oregon criminal law. Specifically, whether Officer Clark's subjective beliefs were objectively reasonable. The question at issue is not whether Mr. Cox actually intended to injure or assault Officer Clark, but instead, whether Officer Clark's belief that Mr. Cox posed a threat was objectively reasonable. Applying that narrow analysis, it is my conclusion that Officer Clark's use of force was justified and his actions cannot be charged as a crime. Therefore, I am declining to issue charges against Officer Clark.

Oregon law provides protections from criminal liability to peace officers when using force to effectuate an arrest or in self-defense, actions that are part of their sworn and authorized duty to the public. The law grounds those protections in the concept of reasonableness with respect to the use of force and the extent of force used. Statutory protections relating to the use of force in connection with making an arrest and in self-defense and defense of others are characterized as justification defenses under Oregon law. Peace officers have a legal right to arrest persons for criminal acts, including during an unlawful assembly and when a riot has been declared during a protest. Probable cause may exist for those committing the violent acts, as well as for those persons who remain unlawfully assembled. Officers are legally allowed to use physical force in order to effectuate those arrests under current state law.

ORS 133.235 authorizes a peace officer generally to make an arrest for a crime and provides that "a peace officer may use physical force as justifiable under ORS 161.245 and [House Bill 4301]". ORS 133.235(4). The statute expressly authorizes the use of force in connection with an arrest, but limits that use of force as outlined in the statutes governing justification defenses. Justification defenses are governed by ORS 161.190–161.275. It is the state's burden to prove beyond a reasonable doubt the force was not justified.

House Bill 4301, Sec. 7, states that, among other reasons, a peace officer may use physical force upon another person only when it is objectively reasonable to make a lawful arrest when there is probable cause to believe the person has committed a crime or when the officer believes a person poses an imminent threat of physical injury to the peace officer. A peace officer may only use a degree of force that the peace officer reasonably believes necessary to make an arrest or to prevent physical injury. House Bill 4301 further states if the peace officer has a reasonable opportunity to do so, the peace officer shall consider alternatives such as verbal de-escalation or give a verbal warning to the person that physical force may be used and provide the person with a reasonable opportunity to comply.

ORS 161.245(1) provides that "a reasonable belief that a person has committed an offense means a reasonable belief in facts or circumstances which, if true, would constitute an offense."

ORS 161.209 provides that a person is justified in using physical force in self-defense "from what the person reasonably believes to be the use or imminent use of unlawful physical force" and limits the amount of force that a defender may use to "the degree of force which the person reasonably believes to be necessary for the purpose." That is, under the statute, a person's use of force is justified as self-defense if 1) the person holds an objectively reasonable subjective belief that unlawful force is being used against them and 2) the person reasonably believes the degree of force used was necessary to defend themselves.

The investigation in this case was conducted by Portland Police Detective Jeff Sharp. I have reviewed the investigation and in addition, all materials submitted by Mr. Cox. The reader is referred to the actual reports for a full account of the investigation, the following is a summary.

The night of August 31, 2020, Officer Thomas Clark was on duty as a member of the Portland Police Bureau's Mobile Field Force (MFF) in the area of NW 12th Ave & NW Glisan St where a protest demonstration was occurring involving a large crowd of people. Members of the crowd threw projectiles at police, including paint balloons and rocks, and shined high-intensity lights at officers. Several fires were started by protestors that had to be put out by the fire bureau, including members of the crowd lightening a fire in a dental office and then burglarizing the business. The Portland Police Bureau declared the protest event an unlawful assembly and riot. The PPB sound truck announced that declaration to the crowd and provided instructions for people to leave the area. The sound truck further warned the crowd that persons who remained in the area would be arrested and force may be used against them. This announcement was repeated at least eight times before police took any action was taken against the crowd.

Tyler Cox was in the intersection at NW 12th Ave & NW Glisan St with a group of people who remained in the street despite the sound truck's warnings. Tyler Cox was dressed in a similar manner to the rest of the crowd, including all black clothing, black gloves, a black helmet, and black backpack. After close to twenty minutes had passed, providing ample time for people to leave the area, the MFF was ordered to move in and arrest the people who remained. Video evidence of the event shows Officer Clark begin to move forward towards the protestors still in the street. He initially focuses on a male carrying a skateboard. As Officer Clark approaches the male, video shows Mr. Cox begin running alongside Officer Clark in a paralleling motion that caught Officer Clark's attention. Officer Clark then turns and moves towards Mr. Cox to arrest him for Interfering with a Peace Officer as Mr. Cox had failed to comply with police orders to disperse and leave the area. Mr. Cox attempts to run away from Officer Clark. Officer Clark grabs Mr. Cox by the shoulders and as he does so, Mr. Cox grabs the top of Officer Clark's vest. Officer Clark takes Mr. Cox to the ground. Once on the ground, the video shows Mr. Cox struggle with Officer Clark, kneeing him, and putting his hands up into Officer Clark's face knocking Officer Clark's helmet off of his head. Once Officer Clark's head is exposed, video shows Officer Clark delivering three to four punches to the area of Mr. Cox's head (the exact point of impact is not visible on video), as Mr. Cox continues to resist arrest and use force against Officer Clark. Once Mr. Cox stops resisting, Officer Clark stops hitting him. Additional officers arrive to assist taking Mr. Cox into custody. While Mr. Cox is still on the ground, video shows Officer Clark attempt to remove Mr. Cox's helmet by pulling on it, but Mr. Cox's helmet does not come off. Once in custody, Mr. Cox was taken to OHSU for medical evaluation and then was released to the police. From this incident Tyler Cox reports the following injuries: Concussion; hematoma to the left side of his head; several cuts, scrapes, and bruises to his head, face, and arms; soreness of his head, neck, and back; and sprains of his left elbow and left shoulder. Mr. Cox submitted photographs of himself following the incident which showed some abrasions along his hairline and in the center of his forehead and a scrape to his elbow.

In this case, there are three points where Officer Clark uses force against Mr. Cox in this incident. The first use of force is Officer Clark grabbing Mr. Cox and taking him to the ground. The second, is Officer Clark punching Mr. Cox in the head. The third, is Officer Clark attempting to remove Mr. Cox's helmet. The analysis in this case focuses on whether Officer Clark's subjective beliefs were objectively reasonable. As such, the question at issue in this case is not whether Mr. Cox actually intended to injure or assault Officer Clark, but instead, whether Officer Clark's belief that Mr. Cox posed a threat was objectively reasonable.

Regarding the first incident of force used against Mr. Cox, Officer Clark had probable cause to arrest Tyler Cox for Interfering with a Peace Officer as Mr. Cox had failed to comply with police orders to disperse and leave the area. Officer Clark decided to arrest Mr. Cox based on that probable cause. As Officer Clark tried to arrest Mr. Cox, Mr. Cox attempted to run away from Officer Clark. As Officer Clark grabbed onto Mr. Cox, Mr. Cox grabbed onto Officer Clark in return and continued to try to get away. At that point, Officer Clark was interacting with a resistant individual. He took him to the ground to gain control over Mr. Cox and effectuate the arrest as quickly as possible. Mr. Cox asserts that Officer Clark picked him up and body slammed him intentionally onto the curb. The video does not support this assertion. The video shows Officer Clark grabbing and turning Mr. Cox before pushing him backwards to the street next to the curb. There is no evidence to suggest Officer Clark acted intentionally to harm Mr. Cox, or that Mr. Cox was intentionally thrown down onto a curb. Under these circumstances, Officer Clark's use of force on Mr. Cox was reasonable to stop Mr. Cox and take him into custody.

Once Officer Clark and Mr. Cox were on the ground, the second incident of force used against Mr. Cox occurred. On the ground, Mr. Cox continued to resist Officer Clark. Mr. Cox kneed Officer Clark, and pushed his hands up into Officer Clark's face. This action knocked Officer Clark's helmet off of his head. Mr. Cox asserts that Officer Clark's helmet was not secured properly, suggesting he used little force to knock the helmet off. Video shows Officer Clark running before taking Mr. Cox to the ground, and then bending his head forward in an attempt to gain control of Mr. Cox. Through all of this significant movement, Officer Clark's helmet remains secured firmly in place. The helmet does not move until Mr. Cox's hands knock it off. Once his head is exposed, Officer Clark then delivers three to four punches to Mr. Cox, striking him on the side of his helmet. When Mr. Cox stops resisting, Officer Clark stops hitting him.

Mr. Cox has asserted that Officer Clark punched him directly in the face at least five times while wearing gloves with plastic reinforced knuckles. However, the videos, medical records, statements of Officer Clark and Mr. Cox, and photographs taken both after Mr. Cox's arrest by law enforcement, and those provided by Mr. Cox himself, do not support that assertion. The available evidence directly refutes that claim. Officer Clark said he was not wearing that type of gloves that day. The video evidence from that night does not show him wearing that type of gloves. Medical records and photographs of Mr. Cox following the incident show that he suffered a single hematoma to the left side of his head in an area covered by both his hairline and his helmet. Small visible abrasions to Mr. Cox's forehead and hairline, near where his helmet padding would likely have been, are present in the photographs he provided. However, these small abrasions are not consistent with his description of being struck in the face five times by a person wearing gloves with plastic reinforced knuckles. The evidence is consistent with Officer Clark's statement, that Officer Clark hit Mr. Cox in the helmet, not the face. Viewed from the perspective of Officer Clark, he perceived Mr. Cox's actions as not only resistant to his efforts to place Mr. Cox under arrest, but also assaultive in that Mr. Cox pushed his hands up into Officer Clark's face and knocked his helmet off. Corroborating this belief, Officer Clark referred criminal charges against Mr. Cox that included Assaulting a Public Safety Officer. Given the environment, and Mr. Cox's behavior, Officer Clark's belief that unlawful force was being used against him was objectively reasonable.

Regarding Officer Clark's belief that he needed to hit Mr. Cox in the helmet in response to Mr. Cox's behavior, Officer Clark was in a declared riot and his task was to arrest people who had refused to comply with police orders to disperse the area. He had run into the crowd and tried to arrest Mr. Cox. Mr. Cox resisted him, put hands into his face, and knocked off his helmet. Officer Clark's head was exposed without protection. Officer Clark was vulnerable without head protection and needed to get Mr. Cox under control as quickly as possible. It was not a situation where Officer Clark would have or should have used any weapons against Mr. Cox, and he did not do so. Instead, Officer Clark hit Mr. Cox three to four times in the helmet in an effort to stop his resistance, and once Mr. Cox stopped resisting and indicated he would comply with the arrest, Officer Clark stopped hitting him. Under these circumstances, Officer Clark's belief that he needed to use that degree of force was objectively reasonable.

Mr. Cox has indicated that Officer Clark's subsequent unsuccessful attempt to remove Mr. Cox's helmet by pulling on it is a third use of force that warrants review. However, video evidence shows that Officer Clark pulled on Mr. Cox's helmet one time. Once it was clear the helmet was not coming off, Officer Clark left it alone. It is not clear from the review of medical records what injuries, if any, resulted directly from this use of force. Further, there is insufficient evidence to show that Officer Clark's action in pulling on the helmet was done with any criminal intent. This action appears to have been incidental to the arrest. It therefore does not warrant further review.

For these reasons, Officer Clark's use of force during the arrest of Tyler Cox was justified under Oregon law. As a result, criminal charges are not warranted in this case.

NOTES

Endnotes

1. Jonathan Capehart, "'Hands Up, Don't Shoot' Was Built on a Lie," WashingtonPost.com, March 16, 2015, https://www.washingtonpost.com/blogs/post-partisan/wp/2015/03/16/lesson-learned-from-the-shooting-of-michael-brown/.

2. "FBI Releases 2019 Statistics on Law Enforcement Officers Killed in Line of Duty," FBI.gov, FBI National Press Office, May 4, 2020, https://www.fbi.gov/news/pressrel/press-releases/fbi-releases-2019-statistics-on-law-enforcement-officers-killed-in-the-line-of-duty.

3. Maxine Bernstein, "Federal Judge Grants 14-Day Temporary Order Barring Portland Police Use of Tear Gas, Except If Lives at Risk," OregonLive.com, June 9, 2020, https://www.oregonlive.com/crime/2020/06/lawyer-for-dont-shoot-portland-suggests-police-should-retreat-not-use-tear-gas-city-argues-plenty-of-limits-already-in-place.html.

4. Noelle Crombie, "Multnomah County DA-Elect Open to Dropping Charges against Demonstrators," OregonLive.com, published June 17, 2020, updated June 18, 2020, https://www.oregonlive.com/crime/2020/06/multnomah-county-da-elect-open-to-dropping-charges-against-demonstrators.html.

5. Joshua Rhett Miller, "Seattle BLM protesters demand white people 'give up' their homes," New York Post, August 14, 2020, https://nypost.com/2020/08/14/seattle-blm-protesters-demand-white-people-give-up-their-homes/.

6. POL Staff, "Portland Commissioner Apologizes for Claiming Police Are Starting Fires," PoliceMag.com, July 24, 2020, https://www.policemag.com/565844/portland-commissioner-apologizes-for-claiming-police-are-setting-fires.

7. "ORS 163.160 Assault in the Fourth Degree," Oregon Laws, Oregon.Public.law, last accessed June 26, 2021, https://oregon.public.law/statutes/ors_163.160.

8. Jonathan Levinson, "Portland Police Officer Charged for Assaulting Activist Photographer at Protest," https://www.opb.org/article/2021/06/15/portland-police-officer-charged-for-assaulting-activist-photographer-at-protest/.

9. Tess Riski, "District Attorney Weighs Prosecution of Portland Police Officer Accused of Punching Medic at August 2020 Protest," *Willamette Week*, WWeek.com, June 25, 2021, https://www.wweek.com/news/courts/2021/06/25/district-attorney-weighs-

prosecution-of-portland-police-officer-accused-of-punching-medic-at-august-2020-protest/.

10. Andy Ngo (@MrAndyNgo), "Watch: Portland Police chase down fleeing #antifa rioters. One gets tackled to the ground and punched in the face. #PortlandRiots," Twitter, September 1, 2020, https://mobile.twitter.com/MrAndyNgo/status/1300691954674483202.

11. Conrad Wilson, "OHSU Nurse Sues City of Portland, Police Officer over Violent Protest Arrest," https://www.opb.org/article/2021/07/01/oshu-nurse-sues-city-of-portland-police-officer-over-violent-protest-arrest/.

12. Maxine Bernstein, "Grand jury finds no criminal wrongdoing by Portland officer who fatally shot man with knife," *Oregon Live*, June 23, 2017, https://www.oregonlive.com/portland/2017/06/grand_jury_finds_no_criminal_w_11.html.

13. Alicia Johnson, "City Council Approves $600,000 Settlement with Terrell Johnson's Family," *Portland Mercury* Blogtown, July 21, 2021, https://www.portlandmercury.com/blogtown/2021/07/21/35271228/city-council-approves-600000-settlement-with-terrell-johnsons-family.

14. The official document included here can be found at https://www.mcda.us/wp-content/uploads/2021/09/Officer-Involved-Protest-Case-Memo-II.pdf.

ABOUT THE AUTHOR

Tommy Clark was born in a remote village in the Philippines and moved to the United States at the age of eleven. After serving in the military, he joined the Portland Police Bureau in June of 2009. Tommy continues to serve in the military as an army reservist, having accumulated more than twenty-two years of service in the U.S. Army.

CPSIA information can be obtained
at www.ICGtesting.com
Printed in the USA
BVHW081728111022
649158BV00008B/1063

9 781955 043670